_Au_

PRACTICAL TECHNIQUES OF
MODERN MAGIC

Marian Green has studied the Western Mystery Tradition and Ritual Magic for many years, and has been the editor of _Quest_ quarterly magazine since 1970. This journal contains articles on all aspects of the Western Mystery Tradition, Natural Magic, divination and personal magical experiences, as well as book reviews and news of esoteric conferences and events.

OTHER BOOKS BY MARIAN GREEN

The Path Through the Labyrinth
Experiments in Aquarian Magic
The Gentle Arts of Aquarian Magic
Magic for the Aquarian Age
A Witch Alone
A Harvest of Festivals
The Grail Seeker's Companion (with John Matthews)
The Elements of Natural Magic
A Calendar of Festivals

All Marion Green's books are available from Thoth
Publications. If you live in the U.K., and wish to receive a
catalogue, send two first class stamps with a self-addressed
envelope to: Thoth Publications, 98 Ashby Road,
Loughborough, Leicestershire, LE11 3AF, England.
Tel: (0509) 210626.
Those who reside outside the U.K. please enclose U.S. $2.00
to offset the cost of international postage

PRACTICAL TECHNIQUES OF
MODERN MAGIC

Marian Green

THOTH PUBLICATIONS

This edition 1993

Thoth Publications
98 Ashby Road
Loughborough
Leicestershire LE11 3AF

First published by Element Books Limited in 1990
entitled *The Elements of Ritual Magic*

ISBN 1 870450 14 0

Printed in England by Booksprint, Bristol

CONTENTS

This book is dedicated to R.W.S.
who has shared so many magical events,
disasters and exciting experiences,
with love and blessings.

THE CIRCLE OF MAGIC

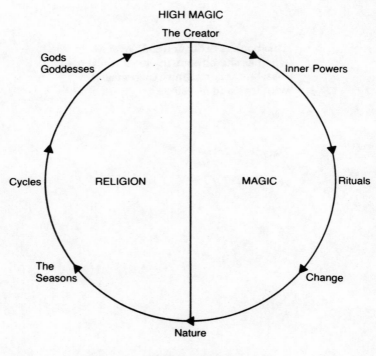

HIGH MAGIC
The Creator

Gods
Goddesses

Inner Powers

Cycles   RELIGION   MAGIC   Rituals

The
Seasons   Change

Nature

NATURAL MAGIC
WITCHCRAFT

INTRODUCTION

Do not meddle in the affairs of Wizards, for they are subtle and quick to anger.

The Lord of the Rings
J.R.R. Tolkien

'Ritual' and 'Magic'– two fascinating words, yet what have they to do with life in the modern world? Are there really wizards and magicians outside films and story books? Can magic work in this technological time? How can a student of such things make progress along the secret roads to master the arcane arts, the hidden traditions, which history tells us flourished in ancient Egypt, in Chaldea, and throughout the Classical world in Greece and Rome?

Certainly the Mysteries still exist. Today the approaches to the hidden paths, the occult skills of mind and hand, the arcane arts of healing and divination, and the use of ceremony and magic rites are more accessible, better understood, and far more widely publicised that they have ever been. In this era of technology and information for all, the initial sources are readily available. The problem for the seeker is not so much how to take his or her first steps along this intriguing road, but which is the safest path, the clearest and straightest highway to the Inner Worlds. Common sense seems to warn that magic is dangerous, and that opening doors to deep levels of perception where hidden powers might manifest on the mundane plane should not be tackled lightly. Yet there is an urge, which many share, to enter the realms of the unseen, to explore those shadowy places outside normal experience.

Curiosity has always been one of the human traits, from most ancient days, which has lured the seeker onwards, through the outer face of religious experience, beyond the common practices of worship to the inner heart of their power and magic. Most of the pre-Christian religions had their magical aspects, and the sciences and technologies of earlier ages worked hand in hand with the priesthood. Theirs was the power to heal, to see the future, to lead the rituals which brought forth the Gods into visible manifestation before the worshippers, to act out the dramas of the lives of the deities, and to be their mouthpiece or oracle, bringing guidance to the mundane folk.

Seasonal festivals brought luck, life and fertility to the land; proper rites marked the passage from childhood to manhood, from single person to married spouse, from nameless infant to named child, and from living being to living spirit, in some other realm, unseen by those who were left behind. Celebrations fêted the returning hero, the successful voyage, the bountiful harvest and the birth of each child, and thanks were offered by ritual, by burning incense, by competitions of strength or skill – most of these things have faded from our calendars. Today our public rituals are limited to the eroded services in the churches, so often bereft of their potent words, their inspiring music, their magical transubstantiations of bread into flesh, wine into blood.

Britain has retained something of her heritage of folk festivals, those pagan survivals of peoples' magic in Morris dances, in Well Dressings, in coronations and state funerals. Here you can discover fragments of a rich ritual life which was once a far more important aspect of all ceremonial occasions, if you learn to read the symbols, the gestures and the half-forgotten actions. Look at the heavy horses pulling the brewer's dray, see their magical brasses, ancient symbols of Sun and Moon, to ward off harm; see the Moon-shaped prints of their iron shoes, nailed above doors to ensure luck, and represent the four aspects of the Moon Goddess, held sacred in every land in the past. Remember the magical arts of the blacksmith, often, in legend, kindred to the devil, who shapes hard iron and banishes ill.

Within our heritage are many jewels of ancient wisdom and power, once carefully guarded secrets held by the priesthood of the land, now diminished to superstitious rites, as half-remembered dances and much-eroded legend, wherein the doings of kings and wizards, poets and heroes make the script for next year's films. All the clues are still to be found, all the power is there for the taking, and nowadays, the training, the practical instruction and the mental disciplines are far easier to approach than they have ever been. What is hard is the long process of training your inner mind, of awakening those hidden levels of consciousness which will gather the scattered clues and weave them again into the bright cloth of the revealed Mysteries. You need to master many practical crafts, of hand and eye, of patience and perseverence, and of recognising the limit of your abilities at that moment. The power is still available, the rites can be rebuilt, re-formed to suit the purposes of the twentieth century, just as they have been for thousands of years, growing and changing like all other living organic systems.

Many people first discover ritual or ceremonial magic in novels or in historic texts about lost brotherhoods, secret societies with mysterious initiations, or books about wizards, ancient or futuristic, who use their strange powers for good or ill, within the plot. Some hear about modern witchcraft yet feel that the coven with its pagan-religious bias, dedicated to the Goddess and the God in their many guises, is not quite the path for them. Others read about the Victorian Order of the Golden Dawn, and perhaps speculate if it still exists, if it would take them in, yet make little progress along that road.

The purpose of this book is to say, 'Yes, some of the ancient Orders do still exist, and accept initiates – but they do not take in completely untrained novices, or those with starry visions of being great Mages.' There are a number of societies in Great Britain with schools or courses of genuine magical instruction which will certainly lead those who persevere with the lengthy novitiate, the boring meditations, the mind-training inner journeys, the mastery of many basic skills, and the attainment of much esoteric knowledge, through the labyrinth into the inner sanctum. But there will never be enough. There will never be an easily available lodge in every town where there are seekers after that sort of magical wisdom, at least not for many decades. Magical Orders that are valid have always been hard to find, few in number, and each can only take in a limited number of newcomers each year. It is not really likely that this situation will change very much, unless those who are seekers now sincerely dedicate themselves to not only becoming competent magicians as individuals, but also taking on the extra, onerous task of being teachers also.

Working within the exalted confines of a properly organised magical lodge is a marvellous and privileged experience. So is being an initiated witch within the circle of a loving and magical coven. These are rare experiences, neither attainable by all nor, probably, sought by all. To earn your place within a magical society, occult Order or Craft coven will require a lot from you. It will require commitment, persistence, dedication and it never has been an easy alternative to a failed life in the mundane world. It will not solve your problems nor sweep them away, but provide you with insights into reality which will probably make your own small perplexities pale into insignificance. It isn't a short cut to power over others, or material wealth, or all the joys of sex without responsibility or love. You will only gain what you have earned, and it is hard work, whether it be power, love, wealth or health, or anything else that you come seeking. Nothing will be given away; nothing can be bought for coin, or coerced from the Inner Powers. You cannot sacrifice for it, except your own time, effort, blood, sweat and tears, and there may be plenty of those, before you have gone very far.

Magic has often been defined as 'Causing changes in consciousness according to will', but today it is seen as a series of mental and spiritual techniques, which, having their roots in the mental levels, flower in the physical world. These many and varied techniques can be learned, in the same way a foreign language is learned, step by step. Gradually control is gained over aspects of the student's inner being so that, through the use of ritual, his purpose is first accurately defined, and then his will is set in motion. Using universal symbols, like those perceived in dreams, the deep levels of consciousness are instructed in what is required, and that objective is set out clearly, by the use of colours, patterns and other correspondences, so that eventually, that which is desired comes into being.

Much of magical training, especially on the path of Ceremonial Magic, concerns learning the symbolic language of the inner realms so that the exact message or instructions are passed on correctly. Magic has a number of parallels with computer technology. A small electronic box, or a talisman, can achieve great results if it is programmed properly, using the right language, symbolic or computer, and from a very small piece of work an enormous objective may result. Make a mistake in the program or miskey the instructions and the result is not what you expect. You don't need to understand what goes on inside a chip to produce the result you want on your computer screen. Similarly, you don't need to understand all the inner processes of magic which make spells work. If you get your instructions and actions right, then the end result will be more or less what you expected.

Ritual is one of the symbolic languages by which we are able to instruct and communicate with the inner realms of magical reality. By use of shape, colour, number, gesture, word or symbol, specific instructions are given to the magician's subconscious mind, and through that a link is formed with the Collective Unconscious, the world, or perhaps universal consciousness. From that instruction work is set in motion and the result will come forth, again perhaps through the language of symbol, if it is a ritual for divination, for example, or in terms of health if it was a healing rite.

Ritual is an experiential art. Writing about it or even watching it will get you nowhere, for real magic is not a spectator sport. You participate, with all your concentration, will and determination, whether you are the newest novice or the most experienced magician. You can only truly learn by doing. In this book I have tried to set out safe and well-tested steps which, if they are followed carefully and slowly, with sincerity and common sense, will lead the greenest novice through the doors to the inner realms and, more important, gently back to his familiar world, as a wiser and more powerful individual. If you think the road to Ritual Magic is your desired path then you will be able to explore it a little at a time, until you are certain of your way.

1 · THE PATHS OF MAGIC

Once you put it into practice, magic is not nearly so dramatic, not anywhere nearly so glamorous as it might have once appeared. Much of it is hard slog and repetition. Results appear without theatricals. This can be disappointing, but at least it is a lot less disappointing than trying something out with no results at all!

Experimental Magic
J.H. Brennan

Anyone who takes an active interest in an obscure and mysterious subject, be it bee-keeping or magic, will face a number of dilemmas, not least of which is, 'What shall I tell the family?'. Although the terror and distrust which once surrounded such subjects as witchcraft and magic have faded to a certain degree, most uninformed and un-involved people treat the mention of anything occult with either grave suspicion or open derision. Those who think they know a little will offer all kinds of advice, describe lurid scenarios based on those seen in horror films, or make suggestions about your morals, sexual habits or desires which are neither accurate nor nice! This is one of the main factors which has tended to preserve secrecy as an important aspect of the Mysteries. The public will either fear or mock those things which they do not understand. This is as true at the end of the twentieth century as it was in the fourteenth.

6

Magic, in any form, is full of paradoxes. It is a collection of ancient arts, crafts and mental skills which seem to date back throughout mankind's recorded history, yet many of the actual techniques are used in the latest psychological therapies and training methods. The paths of magic are essentially secret, yet any good library will have rows of books on all aspects of esoteric thought and occult activities. If you choose such a path you will begin to understand that information on magical lore may be cast like pearls before swine, but only those with any practical experience will really know anything about magic. No matter how much you learn by rote, study or discussion, you will never discover the ways through into the inner realms until you begin the exercises which will change your perception of the world, and so reveal to you what magic is.

You will also be faced with a number of choices, especially early on when you may have little experience and little information to help you decide. The important thing to recognise is that though, at this time, you may take one road rather than another, there is nothing to prevent you, at some other time, walking along the road you ignored before. Just as you can follow one road on a map, or on the ground, come to that, you can only pursue one magical path at a time and have any hope of arriving at your destination.

WITCH OR MAGICIAN?

Perhaps the first decision of this sort which you might have to consider concerns the choice between becoming a witch or a magician. In practical terms, and within modern covens and lodges, it is necessary to know something about both paths, yet it often appears to the outsider that there is no connection. In fact, many people are totally unaware that there is even a choice. Witches have had rather more than their share of publicity in the last couple of decades, not always to their benefit, and ceremonial or ritual magicians virtually none. Even a media interviewer, after questioning someone who professes to be a ritual magician at length, will nearly always turn to the camera or microphone and say, 'I have with me today Miss Blank, and she is a witch' . . .! There is a difference. It does matter.

Ritual magic is not better than witchcraft, or wicca, nor is it opposed to it, nor are these Traditions mutually exclusive. They are different, that is all, and it is safest to choose one or the other to begin with, to see if it suits your aims and nature. Later on, you can turn to the other and, in the light of your enhanced knowledge, explore the alternative.

Ceremonial magic is sometimes called 'High Magic' and witchcraft or folk magic, 'Low Magic'. This is not a judgement, but has derived from historic roots wherein those who were educated, could read and understand the grimoires (or books of the magical arts), often written in Latin or Hebrew, tended to follow the ritual systems, whereas the ordinary folk, unlettered and living closer to Nature, practised much simpler, more intuitive arts and spells, and this became known as Low Magic. A modern concept is that Low Magicians practise their crafts squatting around a cauldron in a forest glade, and High Magicians refine their ceremonies within elaborately constructed temples, wherein they reach upwards to their higher selves. Both work, both provide a wide variety of genuine magical experiences, but each path suits some seekers better than the other. Men and women can be witches, they can equally be ritual magicians, many of the best have trodden each path at a different part of their search for wholeness. But to begin with it is vital to choose only one way and follow that sincerely, for at least a year, before retracing your steps and trying the alternative road.

There are a number of factors which can influence your choice. The first of these is initial 'gut reaction'. If you long for the drama of the incense filled lodge, or your path is that of the Goddess, worshipped out of doors within the firelit circle, you will already have a goal to aim for. If you aren't so sure, perhaps you can think about your choice of a group or a solo journey. Certainly many of our traditional village witches were lone practitioners of their ancient arts, yet we also have a tradition of individual wizards like Merlin or Gandalf. (In magic a legend is just as valid a source of knowledge and concealed wisdom as is 'historical' fact.) Where you live will have some bearing on your possible choice, too. Those in cities will be closer to the location of magical lodges or established covens which, like every other study, flourish where there are enough people to make them work. People do actually travel long distances to attend study weekends or regular meetings, so this is not an absolute necessity. However, as a novice you will need to gain the best training you can discover, for though you will have to learn most of the arts alone in the privacy of your own home, being able to meet others, share your new knowledge, listen to experienced teachers and ask questions will hasten your journey along the path considerably.

HASTEN SLOWLY

There are no short cuts to gaining the infinite powers that well-performed rituals can bring, it takes many years of dedicated effort to learn the arts of mind and body, and to make the subtle inner links with your spiritual, eternal self through which all acts of magic will work. Any system which promises to speed up your progress along the path can lead to danger and psychic disturbances, so be very careful before committing yourself to any form of 'instant enlightenment'. The powers you may learn to control will firstly affect you, opening up doors to perception, both of the material world and of the inner levels. Unless this process is slow and gentle it will cause most unpleasant upheavals in all aspects of your life. Control is the key word in practical magic, and it is only gained step by steady step. Because you will be gaining control of the subtle, hidden processes of your own mind, any leaps into the dark you make will possibly take you beyond your present ability to cope.

To hasten slowly, on any magical path, is a very necessary factor. Any decent school of magic will ensure that each student gains and consolidates his inner and outer skills fully before tackling more advanced work. Any well-written textbook of practical occultism should be studied one chapter or exercise at a time. It really doesn't pay to glance at the first chapters in such a book and then try out the exercises at the end, totally unprepared. You would find yourself in as much trouble as waking up in control of a huge and powerful machine which you have no idea how to stop or steer. You could become really frightened, and within the levels of your consciousness which you had deliberately awakened, no one else could enter to help you.

SYMBOLISM

You will also become aware of the paradox concerning spiritual advancement, which is gained by performing a number of physical actions, using practical tools, solid equipment and material resources. You will have to understand fully the importance of symbolism, so that your workings attract the attention of the kind of energy you require. It takes a long time to remember the lists of correspondences, which act as inner telephone numbers, but these are essential to contact and ask for help from specific powers. Using the potent language of symbolism, you will be able to focus your own will on the purpose of your ritual, and you will link in with the particular angel, power, force or energy which can turn your desire into reality. If you get the 'code', 'number' and 'extension' absolutely correct, then you will be in direct touch with the help you need. It does not guarantee that the power will help you, just as a ringing telephone will not always be answered, or can be engaged, or out of order!

You will have to accept, to begin with, that the strange activities, the use of symbols, dressing up in extraordinary regalia and calling upon invisible entities, dwelling in other planes of existence, can, in fact, produce concrete results, but the more attention to detail you can apply, the more practical experience you get, the more your acceptance will turn into knowledge. That is the true path to power. It is not a matter of believing things so that the strength of your faith makes things happen, but of allowing your disbelief to be held in abeyance until the magical work has been done and the passage of time allows the physical results to be seen. The traditions of magic and the various techniques are all extremely ancient. If they didn't produce results they would have been abandoned long ago. Most of the arts, crafts and skills have certainly changed, they are taught in new ways and expressed in modern terminology or jargon, yet each has very old roots, which can be traced back to their origins.

Because the symbols used in the language of magic are ancient they are also common to many traditions. We may not be able to prove that the original home of all magical technologies was long-lost Atlantis, except intuitively, but close study of a number of different traditions will reveal a great deal of common ground, shared symbols and practical work. These have changed little through the long ages because they work. Our circumstances, life styles and environments may have changed, and the way we communicate, think and understand the inner realities may have evolved from those of our distant ancestors, yet we still can benefit from the timeless arts of healing, divination and use of magical power that were born in the earliest days of mankind upon Earth.

EXPLORATION AND EXAMINATION

There are many avenues which the aspiring magician may explore. Whichever path is selected it will be found to be long and convoluted. There is a great deal of material to be comprehended on all levels, and not merely learned by rote. Myths have to be quarried for their inner meaning as paths to initiation, legends peeled apart for the wisdom in their layers of history, fact and inner truth. Traditions from many lands need to be investigated, for the path which starts nearest to home may not be the one for which you are best suited, nor should students set off on the most remote way to the inner worlds because its strangeness alone is the attraction. Feel, reach out with intuition rather than logic, sense old longings, unexplained affinities with other land or their mythology and culture, recall childhood dreams and memories, strange aversions or feelings of kinship. There may well rest the beginning of the long road, remembered from a previous life, or foreshadowed by a karmic link.

You will need to examine your motives and the principles you hold dear. No true magical path will make you reject, out of hand, a firmly held religious faith, nor ethical or moral standpoints. You may find you explore your feelings in these fields more deeply, and that your orthodox views are changed in the light of personal understanding, but no valid school will force you to abandon them. You will need to accept certain bases before any magical work will make sense, however, but this is unlikely to conflict with common sense. The first concept which will have to have some meaning for you, though you may not actually understand it, is that of some Creative Principle from which the power of change ultimately flows. This can be comprehended as a God or Goddess in your own mind, or a nameless, formless energy, as you will. But in all sincerity such a concept must be real for you or your magic will have no basis at all. You will also eventually need to be able to accept the immortal aspect of your human nature, a soul which is evolving though many lives.

KARMA, REINCARNATION AND RELIGION

The twin aspects, one of Deity and the other of the Immortal within, weave the tapestry of practical magic. The ethics and responsibility which come when magical arts are brought into play revolve around the interaction of these two forces. As you act, so you affect your credit and debit account, called 'karma' by the Eastern Traditionalists. In life we all add to and draw from this inner bank account, but debts of various sorts can be carried from life to life, as can credits. Working with ritual requires each of us to have some idea where we stand in this matter, for much of the work draws upon our inner resources through responsibility, but we may well add credits through healing, advising and performing practical work for individuals or for the world as a whole. It is a subject deserving much meditation and personal understanding. It also raises the whole subject of reincarnation, ongoing relationships through the emotional ties of love and hate, and responsibility for all magical work which may not terminate at our physical death.

Much ritual may have a religious component, in that it could be a celebration in thanksgiving for something, a petition for help, a seasonal ritual, or one concerned with the lives and actions of the Gods, or a consecration. Other religious aspects include divination, wherein the magician is asking advice or guidance from the Divine, probably by the use of symbols like Tarot cards or the *I Ching*, or by direct revelation which is one of the innermost arts of magic. It is by cultivating a familiarity with these seemingly invisible, yet universe-directing powers, that the fruits of magical rites may be seen. Ask for guidance, in the proper way, using the relevant incense, colour, number and ritual form and surely you will coincidentally gain an answer. Magic is an art which causes coincidences, and when you master the skill, these happen about 90 per cent of the time!

Religious ritual is very ancient, dating back, it is thought, to the Stone Age, when early man depicted on his sacred cave walls the successful hunt, the spirits of the slain deer, bears or bison which he hunted for food. He also painted the magician, in his ceremonial costume, with deer antlers and skin, and special garters, performing the sympathetic ritual which would appease the spirit of the slain animal and ensure its fertility, so that it would return as a new creature, to be chased in turn. Some of the oldest yet still most effective magical rites are those in which some desired objective is acted out, by mime, gesture, word or rehearsal, so that the inner realms gain a clear message of what is required to happen in the apparent world. Done correctly, it will work just as well now as it did many thousands of years ago.

MINDPOWER

Other acts of magic are performed entirely mentally, when the trained imagination of the experienced ritual practitioner acts through the stages of what is required, or when a detailed and accurate picture of the outcome of the working is imagined, step by step. As this art of creative visualisation, properly schooled and applied, creates the plan in the mind of the architect, which results in a physical building, so the plan in the mind of the magician creates from the realms of magical reality the changes he seeks in the material world. All magic has a price, however. Just as in physics nothing can be made out of nothing, it is the energy, determination and will of the practitioner which provides the stuff of which the changed reality is made. The arts of magic are called the Great Work, and work it involves. The thought, sweat and tears will all be your own, evoked during the creation of your magical will, just as they would be brought forth if you had built a house with your own hands.

The wisdom takes many years to accumulate. The skills all take time to develop, and the learning processes of all the arcane laws, all the esoteric philosophies, all the practical crafts require many years of concentrated study and gradual gaining of experience. The financial outlay need not be great, for all the best things will be made by your own hand, converted by your ingenuity, sought by your own growing powers of intuition and perception. But the most important things will be the strengthening of aspects of your own character, development of responsibility, understanding and compassion, and none of these will appear overnight!

You will become familiar with the dual processes of thought and meditation so that you can perform those acts of will upon the inner realms which will have their results in the mundane world. You will learn to open and close doors between several levels of your life, keeping a safe distance between the inner and outer realities, and yet understanding and recognising the place for each within any ritual situation. You will learn which of the inner processes can be discussed in public, and which should remain secret. You may learn discrimination so that, when you are offered a choice, you will instinctively understand which is the right way for that moment, which option you should take, and which opportunity to pass by.

Many of the ancient skills, especially those of the mind and consciousness, are emerging within the field of psychology. Neuro-Linguistic Programming (NLP) uses the ancient techniques of inner journeying and visual imagination; the Silva Mind Control uses a form of self-hypnosis; other techniques and therapies exploit the recall and interpretation of dreams. Will is used as a tool in assertiveness training, and many similar popular training methods explore other magical arts. Magic retains many of these mental techniques but uses them in different ways, as doors to inner states where magical seeds may be sown to grow through the changes of time into new realities. Ritual teaches self-awareness, self-control and self-confidence.

13

MAGICAL SCHOOLS AND TRAINING

Although the roots of practical ritual are very ancient, sadly it is not possible to prove that there is an unbroken line of initiates of any tradition stretching back through time. Wars, disasters and movements of peoples, revolutions and mass migrations have mixed up the straight descent of any ancient Law. Certainly there are a number of modern teaching organisations and magical societies whose work is firmly founded on these timeless traditions, but unbroken lines of blood, or learning, or regular ritual can never be said to have continued through all the long aeons. What has happened, however, is that through the ageless links of reincarnation, the trained recall of the magical priests, and the arcane arts of divination and mediation, true aspects of these earliest traditions are being brought to light. Part of the work of many modern orders is that of reclaiming the inner lands and the long-lost sacred sites the world over, so that their concealed wisdom and power may be used and comprehended by the practitioners of today.

This is not true of all organisations which announce themselves in the occult press. One of the first skills it is important to master is that of discrimination, because it might seem fun to glance through the small adverts in some esoteric journal and find that a number of strange and flamboyant-sounding secret societies are touting for new trainees. Most of these are harmless, and some are run by genuine seekers who have chosen the onerous task of leading an occult fellowship as a way of advancement and self-awareness. Some of these self-appointed leaders have received part of their training in a recognised school and what they have to offer may be of great help to other newcomers, but some, having read a few books, have decided that it is a short cut to power or wealth. These are the groups which are most dangerous for the untrained beginner. Because the leaders have had no actual experience of the situations that ritual can cause, when the upheavals, the psychic disquiet, the opening of doors of perception occur among their flock, they simply do not know what to do. The usual reaction is to point to the visions appearing in dark places and blame them on groups of 'black magicians' who are threatening them because the black magicians envy their power and knowledge. The opposite is actually nearer the truth, however, because it is they who are open to the darker, unschooled aspects of their own being, and those of the untrained novices they are trying to con.

A properly set up training group will be well aware of the strange things that happen when magical work is begun, for they know that without this strangeness there is no magic either. Through experience, however, they will be able to steer their students safely through the rough water, and guide them around the dangerous shoals which populate the newly awakened mind.

It is for this reason that gaining at least two or three years instruction within a recognised magical school or course of postal training is worth the time, effort, cost and personal inconvenience. On your own, you can force yourself to study from books alone, perhaps taking the works of one particular modern author and working step-by-step through the magical exercises and practices on your own, but this requires enormous discipline and dedication. Those two mental attitudes are often the hardest to sustain, for many of the initial arts are tiresome and repetitious. Meditation, which will become part of your daily life if you are serious about any form of magic, is often tedious and unrevealing, until the mental knack which permits a change of inner focus to take over can be caused to happen at will. There are techniques which will open these doors of perception for every student, but again, a personal teacher would lead you to them faster than a steady plodding through the collected works of Dion Fortune.

The skills of magic are concerned with control. Initially it must be gained over the various levels of awareness which you must be able to enter at will, so that you can visit the inner realms of symbolic reality; but more important, so that you can return to the everyday world with your memory and consciousness intact. It is a tiny mental step yet some students, who do not have correct guidance, or who have flitted from school to school without mastering this essential skill, can waste several years before the inner 'click' of the door opening is perceived. There is a knack to it, once gained, never forgotten, but without it you have no hope of making real any of the other aspects of magical work. Later on this same self-discipline and control is extended across a wide span of aspects of the work. The persistence to continue with mastering the basic arts, grasping the significance of symbols, the inner meaning of mythology, communication with the Gods and working with their power for change all follow this initial control over your state of mind.

In earlier times it was taught that the mastery of the symbols and ritual forms would lead the student into the correct mental state, and so it does, but today's serious occult teachers prefer students to be able to meditate, make inner journeys, understand mythology and its power before going on to the more ceremonial parts of the study. Both approaches suit some individuals but from my own experience, I feel that an ability to direct your mental state will produce safer and more coherent results than a head full of lists of correspondences, learned parrot-fashion, without understanding. In practice, both methods are used, more or less hand-in-hand, but without the mental control a novice may not be aware of what he is really trying to achieve, because he cannot perceive or intuit what is happening around him on the subtle, magical levels. Without conscious mind-focus these are invisible and incomprehensible to him.

In historic times, the solo magician tended to have developed from the religious hermit. These individuals usually sought lone sanctuary in the wilderness where they could be close to nature, and pray constantly for what ever good they supported. They were often known for their wisdom, their healing abilities and their skill of seeing into the future, none of which is exactly likely to have endeared them to the church of their day! Before the Christian era in the West there were Druid priests, again famed for their knowledge of the stars, their ability to communicate with animals, heal, prophesy, divine and perform magical spells. Although these priests usually gathered together into Groves, some of them certainly would have wandered about the land offering help to those in need, settling legal disputes, teaching the history of the tribes and the great deeds of the heroes of the past. The mythical and historical Merlin seems to have had many of these attributes, being an adviser to the king, and a healer, wise man, prophet and magician, famed throughout Europe.

As well as the individual wizards there were village witches who, unlike the modern, coven witches, inherited their knowledge through the family, much as the baker's children became bakers, and the blacksmith's son became a blacksmith. They retained aspects of the old Druidic magics, the skills to heal with herbs and by laying on hands, both people and animals; the power to foresee and predict events at a distance; the crafts of spell making and potion brewing; the power over life and death, inherent in the knowledge of herbs – some will heal, some will kill. Euthanasia was part of their repertoire in the days before anaesthetics and antibiotics! In a few parts of Britain some old families have retained some parts of this pagan, peasant priesthood, and conduct the arts and crafts

16

of the wise as they have always been practised, in the remote hills and secluded villages. They celebrate a cycle of dramatic seasonal feasts with the whole population of their area, they practise the old magics, linking them to their native landscape, but they retain their secrecy and do their work privately, as did their ancestors during the persecutions.

During many ancient eras whole schools of magic flourished, standing beside the various pagan priesthoods of the time. These taught the mystical philosophies, the occult techniques of far-sight, healing, communication with the inner realms, alchemy, and the potency of cooperation on magical and ritual occasions. Fragments of their secrets have come down to us, often hidden in the complex formulae of alchemical texts and in the traditions of the Craft Guilds, from which sprang the modern speculative Freemasonry, and the Rosicrucians.

In more recent times wholly magical Orders have emerged, the most famous of which is probably the Hermetic Order of the Golden Dawn at the end of the nineteenth century. Within its Lodges the best magical minds of the era studied and practised complex rituals, then squabbled and parted company. Other Orders were founded from fragments of the Golden Dawn's works, some of which continue to this day, both in Britain and the USA. The most prominent was perhaps the Society of the Inner Light, founded by Dion Fortune, and this still runs a school based on the principles of the Christian Qabalah. Also, the Servants of the Light Association, which provides excellent teaching to many students worldwide, was formed through the work of W.E. Butler and others.

Students and initiates of some of these earlier Orders have gone on with their work and founded a number of other Orders, societies and schools, and individuals have become noted writers, lecturers and practitioners of the magical arts. The outer aspects of such works may be found in any good bookshop, or advertised in the widely available occult press.

It takes only a small step to move from the wholly mundane world into that which admits of magic, sacred ritual and secret arts. It should never be a step taken in ignorance, in a desire for instant power or greed, or as an escape from the troubles of the everyday round. Entering the Unseen realms should be taken as seriously as entering into the state of marriage, or a career, or a religious faith. The decision should be taken consciously and not drifted into as a passing whim. It is a dangerous path for it will uncover many weaknesses in the student's character, it will show him his dark and repressed side clearly in the light of enhanced knowledge, and there is no hiding place from wisdom. It is also the path of joy, of fulfilment and of service to the Most High. The door before you is opening now.

2 · STARTING SMALL

The idea that for a tyro to inadvertently or presumptuously say a 'Word of Power' or inscribe a 'Mystic Sign' is to risk his being blasted on the spot with terrible supramundane forces, belongs strictly to the fiction writer's imagination. One gets as much out of magic as one puts in to it. And in the initial stages, having put little into it one is hardly likely to get uncontrollable forces out of it. . . . For the experienced magician, however, it is possible to get out far more than he puts in.

The Practice of Ritual Magic
Gareth Knight

Ritual forms part of our everyday lives. We act out a series of events because we intend a desired thing to come about. For example, we switch on the electric kettle, find a cup, spoon into it instant coffee powder, and when the water is hot add that, and perhaps milk or sugar to taste. What we end up with is a cup of coffee, not a jar of raspberry jam or a sponge cake. In the coffee making, we do not have to know what electricity is, or how it is produced, we do not have to grow and harvest and process the coffee beans, nor make the cup. What we do need to understand is that for a cup of coffee we will require the cup, the water and its heater, the coffee flavour and so on. Ritual is similar. A series of known symbols, words and gestures are set out in a particular order and the end result (which may not manifest as fast as instant coffee) which we aimed for will come to pass. We need to plan the process, find the right equipment, allow time for the sequence of events to take place, and actually play our own part in making it happen.

In making coffee, as in magic, there are dangers. A careless action with a kettle of boiling water can cause serious scalds. Too much coffee can keep us awake all night, too much sugar can rot our teeth. We can spill an expensive jar of coffee mix, or drop the lot on a new carpet and spoil that. Most of these things don't happen, because we are aware of the dangers and take care. The same kind of thought needs to be applied to magical work. If you think what you are doing, make plans, clear the working space, select the right equipment and place it securely, no harm will come to you. If you are careless, unthinking or get distracted then you might cause harm to yourself or your environment. A hot incense burner can burn you or the carpet, just as scalding coffee can. Too much magic can also keep you awake at night, and cause uneasy dreams. Being cautious and thinking things through can save a lot of heartache and worry until you are proficient in the old arts.

Again, if you have the good fortune to be taken under the wing of a competent teacher, or you are learning step-by-step from a reliable school or source book you will be in safe hands. Those in greatest danger from magical mistakes are those people who are at risk in the ordinary world too. If you study each step before you take it your journey may be slow but you will arrive in one piece, whereas if you plunge in with your eyes closed you can endanger yourself and those around you. Magic is neither for the faint-hearted, for you do need courage and determination, nor for the rash and foolhardy, for they may rush in where angels fear to tread. The realms of inner life, the place of dreams and intentions is a landscape which careless magical acts can destroy, just as thoughtless driving can wreck the car and whatever it collides with. The inner realms are where you find peace, where your plans for the future are created, and where the fruits of all your lifetimes are harvested as stored memories for future reference. Act without consideration and these secret essences of what you were, are, and will be, can be mixed and destroyed.

COMPANIONS AND RELATIONSHIPS

Anyone can perform acts of ritual magic and achieve successful aims. Some people will find it much easier than others. You do not have to have a university degree, but an enquiring mind and a lot of common sense. If you are able to find a companion to walk with you in these strange lands you will have an advantage over those who must walk alone. It is best if your partner is someone of the opposite sex; a friend and helper rather than a sexual partner is what you need to begin with. The relationships within magic may seem strange in terms of those encountered in the ordinary world, because you are working on a level of great trust and confidence above all other considerations. There is a different sort of interpersonal chemistry at work within a coven or ritual lodge to that encountered in other groups. It is vital that you feel at ease among your occult companions, that you are your 'true' self, not hiding behind the defensive mask worn in the outer world. You have to trust those you work with, and they must trust you. When you are handling power it will press hardest on the weakest link in the chain, so all must share and take the strain. False arrogance will be your downfall.

In the past there were separate schools of religion and magic for men and women, but today, although the Women's Mysteries and the Solar Tradition do both exist as independent traditions, these are for more experienced practitioners. As in all things, it really helps novices to maintain a balance of sexual polarity, for both men and women have their strengths and weaknesses. Women are the receivers of intuition, inner guidance and diviners, whereas men can best work with the practical side of ritual, making sure the rite is held firm on the outer level. Working in equal partnership leads to a great harmony of power and effectiveness. Obviously we don't live in a perfect world, and often beginners have only one friend who is willing to work with them, and he or she may be of the same sex. It is better to work with someone, but you can often start as a pair and ask to meet up with like-minded folk of the opposite sex to help the work. Magic does not have to involve sexual relationships. Many witches and magicians are happily married, or totally celibate, that is their choice. Only novels or the tabloid press go on about sex rites; real magicians soon learn that they have other things on their minds when it comes to the Great Work!

What does develop between those who share their ceremonies will often go deeper than conventional friendship, for it is built upon mutual trust, respect and honour. It is so different from other relationships that it is not likely to interfere with marriages or other partnerships. What can happen, of course, in an unbalanced group, is that power struggles develop, and the desire for position or preferential treatment brings out the worst in people's characters. It is personality clashes and mean-mindedness that destroys the harmony of groups far more often than any esoteric forces they may have brought to light. All kinds of arcane work will act as a magnifying glass upon the personality of the individuals concerned. If you are greedy or power-seeking, if you are self-confident or feckless, within the occult working these traits may be expanded. You may find others don't like you for what you are, and you might not like them. Perhaps it is a hint that you need to grow, to deal with your basic self first, before submitting it to the enhanced scrutiny of magical folk, or that you need to master tolerance and sympathy. Ideal groups do not often exist; you will have to grow to fit whatever you are offered and, as magic is much concerned with change, be willing to alter your outlook or desires to fit in with the group. It can be a painful process for any adult who has convinced themselves that the agonies of 'growing up' are long behind them, and it can open your eyes to the human condition.

SELF-DISCOVERY

The earliest exercises in any good school of magic will insist that you examine who you are, where you are going, what you most desire, and what aspects of your inner being you have to help you. These exercises may not be pleasant, but they are necessary, and should not be missed out because they hurt or seem difficult. Unless you can see yourself very clearly, you will have no standard by which to compare others with whom you make magic. This is part of the secret occult training; you alone see your own abilities, some on the outer levels and some on the inner. Magically, men and women are not the same. In a working group the natural differences will be exploited, so that the men hold together the physical side of the working whereas the women bring through and transmit the power. There is plenty of room for both, each playing a vital, equal but different part. There are all-male and all-female groups, but the way they work is not the same as a mixed group, and beginners should always try to work with people of both sexes. The relationship within the lodge may be close and loving, but on the whole it will not be sexual, at that level.

The objective of all magical training is at first to make contact with, and later to enhance the Higher Self of the magician. In terms of Jung's psychology, this inner aspect of each of us is called the Animus in women and the Anima in men. It is immortal and through it our ongoing memories of past lives may be reawakened. It is wise, for it has all our memories and experiences, but it is closed off from our normal waking consciousness by a fine, yet normally unbreachable veil. The reason that the arts of meditation and creative visualisation are so important is that these ancient skills allow us gently to lift a corner of this veil screening our inner selves, and to let it fall back into place, like a fire curtain, when it is not needed. By reopening this entrance to our Eternal selves we open a channel for wisdom, power and magical achievement, and this is what causes our spells to work, our divinations to reveal aspects of the future to us, and brings forth guidance and healing. What magic does for us is to give us total control of the process, whereas others who have not been trained can have this shield broken through illness, use of drugs and by ill-applied psychological techniques. This tearing and ravaging of the veil leads to mental illness, depression and uncontrolled psychic intrusions into waking consciousness. Some forms of madness are certainly the manifestation of mistreated inner selves, not often caused by playing with magical techniques, but sometimes so.

EXERCISES

Although most novices are not aware just how potent the forces of magical work can be they should take heed of the warnings, and always hasten slowly along the winding path of power and light. It is for this reason that the following basic exercises need to be repeated until their effects are fully understood. Each of these should be tried on its own, and detailed notes of what happened, what you perceived and any results should be written down and kept. Only by looking back over the notes of previous weeks and months will you be able to determine your individual progress. Like a child growing up, the stages are not seen from inside, but only acknowledged by observers, or discovered in retrospect.

EXERCISE ONE – BEING STILL

This sounds extremely simple and yet you will probably find it is very hard to do properly. You will need a quiet, warm place, an upright chair and a clock or watch which you can see from your seat in the chair. Shut the door, switch off all distractions and tell the household not to disturb you for about half an hour. Sit down in the chair, in ordinary light, settle yourself so that your back is upright, your head and neck straight, your shoulders relaxed with your hands resting comfortably in your lap. Your feet should be flat on the floor or on a thick book so that there is no pressure under your knees.

Close your eyes and become as physically *still* as you can. Breathe gently and slowly, allowing yourself to relax. *Do not move at all!* At the first break of attention, glance at the clock, then begin again. Become rested, still and relaxed. Listen with all your attention to what you can hear and mentally note it. Mentally feel around inside your body, again noting sensations, tensions, tingles and other distractions. Mentally note these. Put your attention on the outer level of your skin, feel your clothes, your weight on the chair, coolness or warmth about you. Mentally note all these things. Glance at the clock again. Probably only a minute or so will have passed.

Repeat the feeling and sensing exercise, remaining still, breathing slowly and becoming relaxed without nodding off. Try to awaken your inner senses and reach beyond where you are sitting. Stay still for at least five minutes. (It may feel like forever, but when you glance at the clock only moments may have passed.)

Keep at this exercise each day until you can remain still and not be distracted for five minutes at least – ten as maximum at this stage. Jot down your recollections of noise, feelings and so on each day.

EXERCISE TWO – WHO AM I?

Repeat the stillness exercise, but when you have relaxed a little and been quiet for a couple of minutes, ask yourself silently, 'Who am I?' There is no definitive answer, but again, simply remain still and consider the question. It may surprise you that emotions are evoked that you do not expect. Feelings of sadness, loneliness, happiness and strangeness are common. Allow them to happen. You are on your own at this stage, so if you cry or laugh or become very introspective it won't matter.

Keep notes of your impressions, and each day for a week find a new starting point to begin from. You may consider your name, your personal history, your job, family commitments, ancestors and so on, but always allow the ideas, pictures, memories and what have you to flow unchecked past your point of awareness. The more still, relaxed and focused on the exercise you are, the clearer and easier to remember will become the concepts that you tuck into your mental store, to be recorded in your notebook. There is no easy way to master the knack, no short cuts, but constant practice until you succeed. Without continuing, even when it seems very boring and unrewarding, you will never gain the most valuable and basic skill of stillness to be used in magic.

You may well be surprised at the effects even these simple first steps can have. The attempts at complete stillness and relaxation often prove extremely difficult, yet if your attention cannot focus on being at rest you will find all the other exercises impossible. When working in a group this relaxed yet alert frame of mind is imperative during all inner journeys, during the meditative parts of rituals, and at any time when you do not need to speak or move. Being still will actually change your thinking processes into a much more magical mode; it will make meditations fruitful, and the images and impressions of inner journeys far clearer and more solid.

EXERCISE THREE – CHANTING AND SPEAKING

This exercise is best performed out of doors, or somewhere where making a noise will not disturb anyone or cause them to be curious. You won't need to make a lot of noise, but you will need to feel free to express yourself and not be embarrassed. Find a book of poetry or good strong narrative description or even a Shakespeare play.

The first exercise is to begin by humming or groaning aloud the lowest note you can make. Breathe deeply and regularly and hum/groan ten times using all your breath. Next choose a slightly higher note and hum or sing that, concentrating only on singing it gently and as regularly as you can, again for ten breaths. It doesn't matter in the slightest what sort of sound comes out, the important thing is performing the note as well as you can, with all your attention focused on doing it to the best of your ability. The third note may be higher still. Search about until you make a sound which you find pleasant, and do that ten times over. See how you are feeling about the process, and remember to make notes when you can.

Now take the poem or other piece of literature of your choice, and quietly read it aloud. Repeat this much more slowly, pronouncing each word and hearing yourself do it. You are not aiming for volume, or carrying power, or dramatic effect but genuine comprehension on your part of what you read. This is the way that ritual speeches will need to be spoken and listened to, when you get on to real ritual. You must attend to the words, analysing them for meaning, allowing time for them to be understood, and letting them sink into your inner perception.

Again, a simple exercise which will have a far greater impact that you might imagine. Keep at it with different sorts of words, prayers, verses, songs, stories and prose until you are satisfied and really grasp what you are doing.

PREPARATION FOR MEDITATION AND RITUAL

In many books of magical rituals there are a wide variety of Banishing Rites. These have the effect of disinfecting and emptying the area in which any kind of occult work is to be performed, but sometimes no warnings are given as to just how effective these can be. Novices are encouraged to draw magical circles around themselves, night and morning, lest any nasty influence rise up and get them. Certainly there is a need to cleanse the psychic atmosphere if you wish to meditate in a room in which the family have just had a row, or if you are very disturbed by exterior sounds and distractions, but it and only then should a Banishing Rite be performed. Doing them willy-nilly only banishes love, caring, friendship and all the good things from your life, as it will shift the darker energies very quickly. People find that loneliness creeps in, and a dull despair which is often attributed to some dark force, when what is really being detected is simply a vacuum which previously had been filled with sounds and subliminal beneficial energies.

It is worth doing some physical cleaning and tidying up before you settle down to even a simple meditation, for that helps prepare the mind and calm the body. It is worth setting out your notebook and pen, or a cassette recorder if you prefer audio notes. You might like the scent of incense or joss sticks, a dim light to still the atmosphere, and these basic things should all be ready before you begin. You should relax and stretch a bit, even do some aerobic exercises to help you release tension in your neck, back and face muscles so that you are able to sink peacefully into the meditation mode. And, rather than doing a Banishing Ritual, start off with the following simple exercise, which makes you think about your place in the universe, and helps establish your Magical Personality.

EXERCISE FOUR – BECOMING MAGIC

Clear a space in a room or out of doors, and stand balanced in the centre of it with your feet a shoulder-width apart, and your knees slightly bent. Breathe in deeply a few times and allow yourself to become still and calm. Slowly and with full attention, repeat the following phrases. Each has a gesture which will become clear to you as you carry out the exercise.

Say, 'Beneath me is the Earth, Mother of my physical Being'. Wait a few moments, then say, 'Above me is my guiding star, shining forever'. Pause, then say, 'Behind me are the memories I'm freeing', then, 'Before me is the Light I'll discover'. Then, 'To my Right comes the power of Reason', and, 'To my left flows the knowledge of healing'. Pause, then 'Around me is the joy of all seasons' and, 'Within me is wisdom revealing'. This may not appear to be very potent, yet it contains the keys to magical balance and enlightenment. Do try to understand what is implied, and then see how it affects you and your state of awareness.

You can use exactly this wording before a meditation and again at the end to set formal edges to your exercises. Later on you will be able to create your own ritual statements, prayers or invocations, but to begin with stick to the simple phrases above, and gradually you will find that you know what each gesture should be, and the force of the energy you have awoken will stir within you. It can be a strange experience, especially for those people who have doubts about anything happening in magic. What is hardest to accept is that, whatever you do with magical intent, be it of greater or lesser importance, it will have a definite effect, even if you are not yet able to detect it. Be very careful, for this reason, when trying out ritual work. If you are inexperienced only try out those exercises which are designed to train beginners; don't, for your own safety, start playing about with difficult bits of rituals from other sorts of books. Every rite will open some doors, and until you are trained, gently and slowly, to open and close those doors at will, leave them alone.

Later on, if you accept that the path of ritual or ceremonial magic is the one you wish to follow, you will probably make a special robe to wear, clear out a magical circle, learn to bless it and sink deep within the purified atmosphere to reach greater sources of knowledge and inner guidance, but to begin with, it is still a matter of going slowly forward, a step at a time. It may be tempting to dabble, to try out snippets from a variety of sources, mix traditions, symbols and working patterns, but it won't really help you in the long run, because you will simply get confused, disturbed and bewildered, and this may cause you to lose confidence in your self and in the Eternal Mysteries which you desire to study. Take care with these initial steps and the path will be clearer, safer and straighter before you, and your own skills and intuitive abilities will gently develop. You will gain control over your waking life, because you will have confidence, and through recalling and understanding your dreams, you will gain insights into the future, the past and your place in the world, and its evolution.

TUNING IN

The disturbing energies and enhanced perceptions you may discover around you when you start on your occult training have always been there but you have been unaware of them. It is just as if, after listening to a radio for years, someone has given you a television set. Instead of just sounds coming out of the ether to your radio, you now have pictures as well. The sound and light frequencies have always been there, it is just that now you have the equipment to pick up the signals and make sense of them.

Most of real magic is a matter of tuning in to the particular symbols, myths or God forms required by the work in hand. Training is mainly concerned with filling up your personal memory banks with that data, and once you have learned who goes with whom in any given pantheon, what their symbols, colours, shapes and mythical animals are, you have the basic pattern of any ritual for any purpose. It is similar to having a list of television channels from which you can select your future viewing. As with TV, you can really only watch one programme at a time, even if your video recorder is able to watch another on your behalf. You will have to concentrate on one channel, one tradition of magical symbolism and mythology at a time, rather than flitting from one to the other if you happen to forget which God or Goddess fits a particular job, in the pantheon you began with. Homework and serious study are very important so that you won't forget what you need at any given moment.

EXERCISE FIVE – ENCOUNTERING A MYTH

From any book you have read thoroughly, select a single character. It could be a contemporary novel, a folk tale, a legend or a sci-fi epic, but you will need to know quite a lot about the individual you have chosen for this exercise.

Again, shut out the world, sit comfortably relaxed in your upright chair, breathe deeply and evenly, sensing tension departing on the outbreath and breathing in calmness and magical perception. You can use the exercise of 'Becoming Magic' if it helps you to shift your level of awareness. Close your eyes.

Then imagine the character you have chosen standing or sitting before you, seeing as clearly as you can its face, clothes and perhaps surroundings. Wait for it to be fully visible to your inner vision. You can then ask it something about its story and, if you have entered the inner world completely, you will hear a reply. It might take several attempts to get the figure fully into focus, and several more for it to seem willing to reply to your single question. You might well be astonished as to what kind of answer you may obtain this way, if you are willing to persist with the basic exercise until something does happen.

Like the previous exercises, perseverence is needed so that when you begin performing ritual, the thought patterns of seeing, sensing, hearing and communicating with other levels of reality are working for you. Otherwise, you would enter the ritual blind, deaf and out of communication with the very angels or Gods you wish to ask for advice, guidance or practical help. You would not be able to recognise their presence or gain anything useful from the rite. In the above exercise you are 'imagining' the character, and probably also 'imagining' the answer to your question or even the lengthy conversation which follows, but it is very good practice, all the same.

Although these exercises are very simple when you read them, if you have had no experience of magical working, you may be surprised by two things. Firstly, some people find even being still and concentrating for a few minutes extremely difficult, whilst others who have never lost the skills they had as a child find the basic exercises quite easy. Secondly, you may be astonished at what profound effects these initial steps can have. The stillness and inner silence can be unnerving, the sudden awareness of your own breathing and pulse can be strange. The power of some familiar story or legend to awaken a hidden surge of feeling or emotional release can be quite overwhelming, but you do need to recognise that this can happen.

Learn to accept strong feelings, feel free in your reactions and responses, for these add energy to the working out of your spell or intention. You should be willing to accept such emotional out-pourings from your companions, too, without judgement or embar-rassment. These things are clear indications that you are allowing the magical resources within you to have free rein, although you

29

should be fully aware that magical ritual is not an excuse for over-dramatisation, nor for letting forth anger or resentment. Any reaction should be heartfelt and not a matter of acting. If you are not strongly moved by your celebration, spell or religious ritual, you will need to rehearse some of the early exercises until you can enter fully into the Mystery, and permit something to happen to you.

3 · THE CIRCLE, THE SQUARE AND THE SPHERE

Now when you perform a ritual 'with intention', as we say, you will be building up a definite set of thought images, and those of us who possess a clairvoyant faculty can see that these thought images are formed in the plastic substance of astral light. It is these images which form the conducting channels for the inner energies which we call down into our personal sphere.

Apprenticed to Magic
W.E. Butler

Working any kind of ritual requires a ritual space, even if you are alone and simply carrying out a daily meditation, which if you are serious about your studies, you will do, in some form or other, for the rest of your life. This space may be a small area around your chair, mentally delineated and surrounded by a sphere of calmness and light, or it might be an actual temple, a room set aside for magical work. In a separate place all the furnishings, equipment and ceremonial objects may be set out, consecrated and made ready for ritual use. Even though that space is totally dedicated to the work, it will still need to be resanctified every time it is used, not because it might become unholy, but because the practitioner, moving between

31

the worlds of mundane activity and magic, may bring disturbing vibrations with him. We need to be able to enter the magical circle, set aside all disturbing thoughts and replace them deliberately with mystical images, the mental descriptions and the visualisation of which create the vital change in our consciousness, which makes magic work.

THE CIRCLE

The circle, as a magical place, is a very ancient concept. Perhaps the earliest blessed ring was outlined by the dancing flames of a fire, or the flickering light of a simple lamp. The circle is still a place of light, from which darkness of the visible and mental sort is banished. Usually it is still illuminated, at least in part, by a real candle flame, or the light of an oil lamp. This alone can help set in motion that very important change of awareness which gives validity and power to meditations and ritual alike. Unless something leads to this entry into a magical state of mind, all the chanting, wand waving, dressing up, invoking of angels, incenses, symbols and words of power will have no effect. Make that small refocussing of your attention towards the inner realms and anything is possible. Learn to master that state, through regular meditation and hard work, and you will be able to conjure into being your own secret place, the circle of Stonehenge's mighty monoliths, the ring of ancient marker stones from many an ancient site, the guardian trees of the ancient forest, or a pattern of carved pillars from the glorious temples of the Classical ages. Although you may at first be drawn to a simple tradition, if you follow your interest in ritual and work with other people or within a particular group, you may have to accept all kinds of different scenarios used in shared working. It is important to be able to sense that scene, feel it so well that it becomes real around you. Within those mind-built walls will be the focus of your power; from that created scene your pleas for help will be sent forth, and into that sacred space will the answer be returned. If the circle remains 'in your imagination' then it will have no strength to protect your intuitive self, nor will it contain and then send forth your will.

EXERCISE SIX – THE CIRCLE OF LIGHT

Again this is just a matter of sitting completely still, in a dark room with a single nightlight or small candle, placed in a secure and draught-proof holder.

Allow yourself to become quite still and balanced, with your eyes open, relaxing and breathing slowly and deeply. Then light the candle and allow its flame to become steady. Set it where you can see it without strain. Half close your eyes and squint at the flame. You ought to be able to see filaments of rainbow light streaming from the heart of the flame. This is the effect of looking through your eyelashes, but the result is very much like seeing the aura of the flame.

Become aware of the circle of light spreading outwards from that small source. Be aware that it spreads not only sideways, but up and, in theory, downwards too. Become aware that in perfect conditions, for example if you were poised on the top of a high mountain, the light could radiate to infinity, in all directions.

Begin to sense a great sphere of light with you at the centre, as if you were within the flame of the candle. Feel the brilliant edges of that sphere and see them in shining white-gold light all round you. Then close your eyes and continue to see the sphere of golden light, within which are sparkling filaments of rainbow colours, representing the energy within your own aura. Remain quite still within this sphere. Seek out sensations of peace and calmness, quietness and a sense of anticipation.

This is the starting point for many magical journeys you may make in the future and it is a matter of getting this basic visualisation right, so do keep on with it until you get some definite awareness of the sphere of light and its growing power before going on to later exercises. You will not only need to perceive the sphere of light about yourself, but also be able to extend it over a place which you are making sacred for whatever ritual you might perform.

THE FOUR QUARTERS AND THE FOUR ELEMENTS

You will also need to recognise the four points of the compass, or Quarters, and discover a series of things associated with each. Some of these may be physical objects, others concepts, angels, or invisible forces with which you will learn to balance your workings. It is worth buying a small but accurate compass, especially if you intend to wander about the countryside at night. It can be very dark out there, and a back-bearing towards your car or the nearest road can save hours of groping about in pitch darkness.

Indoors, you may be in a position to set out a permanent altar and, if there is sufficient space, the four Quarter points and their associated symbols. You will gradually build up collections of useful candle holders, cups and small dishes, perhaps a wand or two, and a decently sharp knife for cutting these from living trees, gently and cleanly. In the old days most magicians had a ritual sword, and many of us still do, but it is a symbol which can be represented in other ways which are less likely to get the initiate into trouble with the law, if it is necessary to take magical instruments to a ritual away from home. The same applies to the witches' famous 'athames', the black-handled ritual knife. A Swiss Army knife might not look as good on the altar as a black-hilted dagger inscribed with runes, but if you have forgotten the corkscrew, or wish to tighten a screw, it is a lot more practical!

Of course, you *can* send off lots of money to an occult supplier for a complete ritual kit, with all the paraphernalia, incenses and equipment, robes and so on, but it will make your work four times harder than gradually seeking out, making and consecrating all the things you need, perhaps over several years. It will certainly tune up your occult senses, sharpen your inner wits and provide excellent opportunities for you to master some of the practical arts associated with ritual. You will need to make a robe, design a personal pentacle, discover all the various other articles, cleanse and consecrate them. It adds up to a fair-sized cupboard-full, in time, but it should not cost you much money. What you pay with, as you master the practical skills, is quite often blood, sweat and tears, from pricked or cut fingers, and the frustration of having the glass goblet you have so lovingly decorated slip through your fingers and smash on a hard floor just as you bless it with holy oil.

There are dozens of different ways of attributing the elements of Air, Earth, Fire and Water to the four directions, and each one is right – for whoever devises it and works with it. You *can* start from scratch and invent your own attributes but, on the whole, it is easier to start with one of the most frequently used arrangements and change it later if you need to. It is best to look first at the four Elements and what is usually considered magically important about each, and then the basic bits of equipment which are associated with each.

EARTH

Starting with North, this, in most places in the Northern hemisphere, is the place for Earth. This is the hard-standing upon which your magical temple of the mind will be built, and the foundations of all your practical work. Get your relationship with Earth right and other things are easier and more secure. It is also your physical body, which matters a great deal in magic. The old plough-men would say, 'No foot, no horse!'. The magical instructor would similarly say, 'No body, no occultist!'. If you take care of your physical being, learn to love it, feed it properly and cease polluting it with smoke or chemicals which harm it, it will serve as the temple of your magical will, always present, always ready to serve the higher purpose. Accept that magic is served by real things and not imaginary ideals, that the actual physical world is important and the objects you make or acquire for your magical work need to be treated with care and respect, because they are, or soon become, sacred.

The most obvious things which are associated with magical Earth are stones, actual earth or sand, slate or pieces of wood. Crystals, although quarried from under the earth, are actually related to Spirit, the fifth element, and are best used separately, at least to begin with. The symbol to be placed on the altar, your working table, can be the flat pentacle, which may be an earthenware dish, a wooden platter, a round bread-board carved or painted with your representation of your feelings about Earth. It could be a circular marble cheeseboard or even a natural slate or rock upon which you can lay the bread for your communion. You might also like a small pottery dish in which loose material like sand can be kept, or this might be used for the salt, if you use this as a consumable in the communion, which in many occult circles includes bread, wine and salt. A further Earth symbol could be a lamen; this is a small pendant worn on a ribbon or cord around your neck, which could be a natural holed stone, fossil or wooden disc, painted with earthy images, or even a ring of seeds (although by drying and piercing these you rid them of their natural fertility and life) or stone beads. It will depend on how elaborate your intended rituals are to be as to how many and which of these links with elemental Earth you will need. You will certainly discover others as you go along.

WATER

The next element to consider is that of Water. Here you move into the field of the emotions, feelings, psychic abilities of the most basic sort, and the key word is 'control'. Unless you can control your temper or other strong feelings, you will never have the self-control to work ritual with any degree of power. The magical way to gain self-control is not by repression, but by honest and open examination of yourself and by meditation upon your difficulties, which will lead to understanding and so to control. You share this earth with many people and must learn to work for and with others.

As the primary symbol of Water is the cup, chalice or cauldron, you will recognise that you are ready to work with this element because someone who loves you will give you a gift of one. It might only be a coffee mug for your birthday, but it does show someone cares for you. (If you win a set of wine glasses in a raffle, that doesn't count!) When you have such a present given to you then you can seek out the great glass goblet from which to serve the communion wine to your group, or the individual chalice, representative of the Holy Grail and all its Mysteries, for your own work. The best ritual cups are silver or glass as moon and water symbols. They can be any metal that is safe to drink from, gold or pewter, but glass, coloured or plain, or pottery in a watery colour is just as good. You might also seek a small bowl in which water to go on the Western side of your altar may be contained. The chalice should have a stem and be large enough to take a decent drink from. Learn to pass the cup around your companions with both hands, and receive it in the same way. Meditate on why this should be necessary.

Water is usually placed to the West, where in Britain we see the Atlantic Ocean, the setting sun, the shades of autumn in the woods, and the dimming light of eventide. Walk in the rain, or meditate upon a beach at sunset, watch the ever-changing pictures of clouds reflected in river water, or the stars in a deep pool at night. Open up your feelings, and learn to show them honestly. Within a ritual such emotions may be aroused by the very nature of the work. If you give thanks, you may feel elated; if you are remembering someone who has died, you might find yourself crying. Allow this to happen, without fear or embarrassment. In pagan rituals particularly, emotional energy adds to the power of the ritual, and if you participate you must be willing to feel the emotion of thanksgiving, welcoming the Goddess or whatever scenario is being worked.

Water is used to bless the circle, the participants and to ritually cleanse magical equipment during its consecration and dedication to the work. A sprig of leaves or herbs may be used to sprinkle drops about. You will always benefit from a ritual bath or shower before any serious work, cleansing your body and relaxing and preparing your mind. If this is impossible, running clean water over your hands and face could be enough and this ceremonial cleansing can be part of the opening of your rite. If you can use natural spring water rather than tap water, it is nicer and that may be used for the communion drink, rather than wine. You will also benefit by learning where your nearest spa is, or source or drinkable spring water. These sources were very sacred to all ancient peoples.

FIRE

Next you will have to come to terms with Fire, usually symbolised by the real flames of a candle or enclosed glass lantern. You will need to find suppliers of suitable candles for your working. If you are a novice, then ordinary white household candles are the best. Later on you may make your own, or have them made by a member of your group, in particular colours or shapes for the needs of each ritual.

To begin with you will need four safe holders if you intend to place one light at each Quarter, or perhaps just a single candlestick to go on the altar itself, if your rites are to be simpler. You will also need a nightlight holder for the centre of your space. This may have coloured glass and be set in a metal holder or even, if circumstances allow, hung in a set of chains from the centre of the ceiling. Remember, you will need to be able to get to it to light it and change the nightlight. Look out for long tapers which can be used to pass a flame around the circle or light candles which are set in deep holders.

Be sensible with naked flames. Robes should be made of non-flammable material if possible, and in any case, care should always be taken when dealing with fire. A fire extinguisher may not be the most beautiful object in the world, but it could save your life if there were to be an accident, so bear this in mind. The same caution needs to be shown if you are lighting anything out of doors, for a small flame can burn down an entire forest or town, and it takes only a moment's inattention for a spark to fly.

Fire relates to the South, to noon, summer, the Sun God, energy and masculine power. It is encountered in nature as lightning, volcanoes and occasionally 'spontaneous combustion', for example when rotting hay heats up enough to burst into flames. You might discover marsh gas and the strange 'will-o-the-wisps' burning with flickering blue flames as methane gas ignites over stagnant water. Within us, it is thought of as energy, enthusiasm and determination, and is often symbolised by a dagger or sword in ritual. Like flames, sharp blades can be hazardous within a confined magical circle, but it is no use having a blunt blade.

AIR

The last terrestrial element is Air, breath and the power of the intellect. It is dawn, the East, wind, the wand and the sweet scents of incenses, flowers and vaporising oils. Here, it is the mind which is brought into focus, that subtle, invisible force behind all our doings, ruler of dreams and visions, bringer of good or ill health, and ultimate power through which our magical desires are brought from imagination into reality. We have only learned within this century of ways of describing the inner life of our minds and intellects, through the development of the language of psychology. Before, the descriptions of journeys into the inner realms seemed to imply actual physical travels, rather than the magical pathworkings we use to enter the other realms of consciousness and psychic awareness. If you read that a magician 'entered a hill and found himself in fairyland' or 'flew through the air to enter the realm of the King of the Winds', it seemed to imply actual entry to the underworld or real flight, in the days before planes and gliders. We now know these were mental journeys, when the trained and liberated consciousness, deep in meditation, could visit any realm, terrestrial or on other planets, the kingdom of wild beasts, the place of the angelic hosts, just as we do today, in our inner journeys.

To learn the secrets of the wand of Air which controls and directs the True Will, the determined desire of the magician, is the hardest task of all. It might quite simple – determining what your True Will is. Surely it must just be what most interests you at the moment, what you want from life and those around you? In magical terms this is not so. Your True Will has to be the main purpose for your current life on Earth, not just the whim of the moment, the wanting of some object or material aim. You will have to spend many long sessions of deep meditation on this topic, for unless you have some idea of your magical objective all your rites may be in vain. You have to accept that your personal wants are very small compared to the purpose of the universe. It is by looking at the long-term, larger span of things that your individual will may emerge. There is no short cut. Any acts of selfishness, of the 'me first' mentality, with the objective of material wealth and gain above the spiritual purpose, will be met with rejection by those very inner powers on whom you hope to call for assistance. You soon learn you are a part of a greater whole and that all persons, all parts, mankind, Nature, the Earth herself, all rank within that scale of need, and must be considered when you plan any working.

Learn to accept that you are a part of the pattern, part of the great cosmic plan, and you will genuinely gain insight and eventually wisdom, that greatest gift of intelligence applied. Gradually you will learn, through meditation, what you can and can't have through magical work, what kinds of spells work, which lead to greater enlightenment, which give you confidence. Also, only practice will demonstrate when you have overstepped the mark.

SPIRIT

The last element to be considered is that of Aether or Spirit. This is magically symbolised in a variety of ways, by the eternal soul within the practitioner, by the outer circle of his magical working, by the flame of the lamp burning at the centre of his altar, and by the ring on his finger by which he is wedded to his arcane art. The attainment of the right to wear a magical ring, which is worn only during your working, comes only when you have come to terms with each of the other four elements and gained control of that aspect of your own nature, by prolonged and serious meditation.

As with all the other elements, you will need to understand Aether yourself before it will bring you its spiritual force in your working. You may find that this causes you to reconsider your views on your religion. Magicians are not by any means all pagans; many adhere faithfully to an orthodox religion, not following blindly, however, but from free and deeply considered choice.

You will certainly benefit from looking at the Table of Correspondences on pp. 40–41 and when you have understood what each set of correspondences means to you, you should be able to add many further sets of four or five things, animals, God and Goddess names, incenses, symbolic shapes or sounds of your own choosing. Of course, you may well read other lists in other books, but before you simply accept anyone's attributions do give at least a session of meditation to the true understanding of these. Unless you realise why things are associated with a particular element, and feel comfortable with that attribution, you will gain no power from using it. The more you think about these things and aim to really understand them, the

TABLE OF CORRESPONDENCES

Note: There are many different ways of allocating symbols and colours to the four Quarters but the ones given here are suggestions to help you begin your work. Do expand and vary this Table as you learn more.

DIRECTION	EAST	SOUTH
Time of Day	Dawn	Noon
Season	Spring	Summer
Element	Air	Fire
Magical Instrument	Wand	Sword/Dagger
Altar Symbol	Incense	Lamp
Communion Symbol	Scent	Heat
Elemental Symbol	△ (Air triangle)	△ (Fire triangle)
Archangel	Raphael	Michael
Human Sense	Hearing/Smelling	Sight
Art Form	Poetry/Painting	Dance/Drama
Elemental Beings	Sylphs	Salamanders
Polarity	Male positive	Male negative
Exhortation	To Will	To Dare
Greek Wind God	Eurus	Notus
Musical Instrument	Wind Instruments/Harp	Brass Instruments
Colours	Gold/White	Scarlet Red
Mythical Beast	Winged Horse	Dragon
Magical Arts	Divinations	Ritual
God Forms	Sky/Weather God	Sun/Protector God
Meditation Images and Themes	Sky/Clouds	Bonfires/Flames
	Mountain Tops	Volcanoes
	Flying	Walking through Fire
	Sunrise	Sun at Noon
	Wisdom and Knowledge	Energy and Power

TABLE OF CORRESPONDENCES (continued)

WEST	NORTH
Sunset	Midnight
Autumn	Winter
Water	Earth
Cup	Pentacle/Stone
Chalice	Platter
Wine/Water	Bread/Salt
▽	▽
Gabriel	Auriel
Taste	Touch
Music/Song	Sculpture/Embroidery
Undines	Gnomes
Female negative	Female positive
To Know	To Keep Silent
Zephyrus	Boreas
Strings/Bells	Drums/Percussion
Blue/Green	Black/Deep Green
Sea Serpent	Unicorn
Healing	Talismans
Moon/Water	Earth/Underworld
Goddess	Goddess
The Ocean/Rivers	Fertile Landscape
Lakes/Pools	Caves/Rocks
Living under Water	Growing Organically
Setting Sun	Moon/Stars/Night
Healing and Calm	Growth and Life

more powerful they will become within your ritual.

To help you put on your magical personality you will also need to discover or write a series of short invocations of blessing. You will find Exercise Four, 'Becoming Magic', can be used to bless yourself and focus your attention on the purpose of the ritual. Again understand what is being said and make it real for yourself. If you have a robe to wear, or even a simple pendant to hang round your neck, you will begin to notice a distinct change in your feelings as you put these things on. Also, as you sit down to plan the purpose and the pattern of your ritual, mentally going through the lists of things you need, cleaning the space within your working area, and concentrating fully upon the work ahead, you will discover a gentle change of awareness, into your magical self.

Before you go any further you need to learn to know about the eight directions of magic, understand them fully, and be aware which point of the compass relates to which others. Stand still and recognise the four directions about yourself: in front, behind, to your right and to your left. You need also to become aware of the concept of above and below. All these are reflected within the way you see the everyday world. The last two directions of magic are within, towards the centre of your very own universe, and outwards, to the widest circle of experience, awareness or perception you can envisage.

EXERCISE SEVEN – CREATING A SPHERE OF PROTECTION

Stand still and relax, with your eyes closed, if possible (some people cannot balance with their eyes closed). Imagine a circle of whitish-gold light like a huge hoop surrounding you, further out from your sides than you could reach with your arms at full stretch. See it glowing or sparkling, and then let it tumble, pivoting at the level of your hips, making you the centre of a glowing golden ball. Next see the circle which encloses you from in front and behind, glowing golden-white. Let that tumble over to your right, again enclosing you completely in a ball of magical light. Finally, see the circle which surrounds you horizontally, at about waist level, burning and sparkling, paler gold, all round you. Let that too tumble upwards, over your face and down behind you, enclosing you in a great sphere of vibrant light.

Imagine that within this globe is perfect peace, quiet and calmness, that you become more strongly yourself. Then discover that the sphere starts to divide, the inside shrinking, contracting and growing brighter yet, to rest gently deep in your heart centre as a spark of your spiritual will. Perceive the outer levels of the sphere growing vast, spreading across the room, the street, the country, the universe, a shining light of the love, the trust, the joy and the delight in sharing this world with others which you must learn to project. This is a magical defence, although you will seldom need it, and then its power need be held for only a moment whilst it strengthens your own confidence and brings you self-control. Use it at the start of meditations or rituals.

Although these preliminary exercises are frequently found in good books of magical training, unless they are learned thoroughly they will be as useful as a cookery book to the hungry. Magic is a series of practical skills. Begin at the simplest exercises and try them out. Work with what happens to you, understand it, and discover now the time doing your meditations differs from idle moments during the day. Be sure there IS a difference. If you get no apparent change in your perceptions you are getting no magic either!

WORKING IT OUT

Get out your compass and decide where North is in relation to the room you are in. Where then are East, West and South? Are these directions where the walls are, or nearer diagonals, with the room's corners as North, East, South and West? It is important to know this as, when you begin working with the symbolism of the elements and the quarters, you must know which is where.

The direction most often considered sacred is East. Churches, for example, nearly always have their main altar at the East, and most religious acknowledge the point of sunrise, which is generally but not exactly compass East. (It shifts North and South in Britain, in summer and winter, and is only due East at the equinoxes.) East is the place of the rising or returning light, and it is symbolised by the Wand or Lance which flies through the air, the breath of the creator. Opposite is the watery West, place of sunset and peace. If you face East, to your right is the South whose magical symbol is the sword, and to your left is the shield, or pentacle, in the North, so you are an armed warrior, equipped to face the oncoming foe.

If, on the other hand, you work to the pagan sacred direction which is North, the place of the Earth Mother and the eternal star of Polaris, in your right, Eastern, hand you hold the wand, the walking stick,

43

the shepherd's crook, and in your left, the Western cup or chalice. You are at peace, guiding your flocks, and sipping your sacred drink.

Place symbols for the shield, the sword, the cup and the wand in the appropriate places. Get to know these, feel their individual and combined power, even if you are not yet ready to seek out, or make, or refurbish the real items. Meditate on what each means to you, if it is still relevant in this technological time, and if it isn't right any more, what might be better? Magic is an ever-growing and changing system, evolving along with its practitioners.

Recognise the power of each direction in turn. Observe the rising Sun and Moon, and their individual setting places. Feel the wet West wind, the cold Easterlies. Revel in the midsummer heat of the Sun at his height, and the deep, still frosty nights of winter, when the moving, guiding stars sparkle in the ebony sky. Learn to know the constellations, the signs of the zodiac, and the way the Great Bear turns about the Pole Star as the night progresses. In many pagan workings, the sacred focus follows the wheeling stars throughout the year. At Yule, mid-winter, the sacred direction is North, then North-east for Candlemas, then East for the spring equinox, South-east at Beltane, South at Midsummer, South-west at harvest time, West at the autumnal equinox, North-west at Hallowe'en, and back to North at Yule again.

Recognise that if you are to make a circle for magic within a square or oblong room, then either you will have to walk round outside the chairs for the four Quarter officers, if you have any, or the circle will be formed inside a square of chairs, which might make it small, although you can project it out to any size you like, when you set it up. If it can be arranged, it is possible to put the chairs in the corners of the square space, and so form a larger circle in the middle. The altar need not be very big. A small, squarish, upright cupboard covered with a velvet cloth may be just the thing, and it makes a place to store your robes, cup, incenses and all the other necessary items, out of the way. A cheap padlock will keep out intruders!

Out of doors you will have more space to wander about in, but there it is often harder to be certain of the directions, and it is no use chanting some evocative poetry towards the East and then noticing the sun setting in front of you! Learn also to turn clockwise and to walk clockwise to open and set up any circle, and to turn anti-clockwise and walk in that direction to unwind and close down each magical circle. This is important and should not be overlooked. If you aren't able to walk about in your personal space, you will at least need to turn to face each Quarter consecutively as you call upon the powers of the East, North and so on.

4 · BUILDING THE TEMPLE

So with all magical 'props' — the sword, the wand, the pentacle, the circles, triangles and sigils, the lights, the robes, the incense, the sonorous words of invocation and the 'barbarous names' of evocation — all work by a cumulative suggestive process upon the subconscious mind. Such a cumulative suggestion results in what may be termed a mental change of gear, and therefore conforms to our earlier definition of magic as the 'art of causing changes in consciousness at will'

> *Magic: Its Ritual, Power and Purpose*
> W. E. Butler

Ritual magic has many facets, all of which are important, and all of which need to be thoroughly understood by the practitioners. It is rightly stated that the paraphernalia of magic is not necessary to the adept, that true rituals take place in the mind and the subtle, invisible realms until they manifest as change in the physical world, and that a genuine magician can perform his art at any time or place. True though these concepts may be, they overlook the importance of psychological aspects of esoteric work. It *is* possible to produce results by pure mental effort, but it is the mental effort of someone who has spent many years working with the physical instruments, the actual temple, and the real objects with which he interacts to practise his art and refine his techniques. The use of material equipment is a vital factor in the mastery of the invisible arts, and few can really ignore it if they want to make progress in ritual magic.

It *is* important to recognise that the symbolic instruments are not just 'props' but tools which are as important to the magician as the spade and shears are to the gardener. Certainly the magician is working in an extra dimension at that moment, for the magician aims to produce fast results, perhaps in a different place, whereas the gardener works to produce physical results in the same place, but at a later time. Neither the gardener or the magician can make a cabbage grow faster than its conditions will allow! By properly using the symbols which represent the four elements, within the circle made blessed and special for that span of time, the magician is setting in motion a change which, in time, will develop into whatever he has asked for. Often the major effect is upon himself. For example, if he has asked for wisdom or understanding of some problem he may discover the answer in a book, or the words of a friend, or in a dream. If he has asked for some material object, he will find it is for sale in a shop, or is given as an unexpected gift. It won't simply materialise before him in a cloud of sweet-scented smoke!

The equipment of magic acts like a kind of lens, focusing the attention fully on whatever project is in hand. It is for this reason that the correspondences are so important. These are based initially upon the four elements, and then on the seven planets of ancient astrology, best known to most people as the rulers of the days of the week, Moon, Mars, Mercury, Jupiter, Venus, Saturn and the Sun. To each are attributed a long list of colours, numbers, gems, incenses, Gods and Goddesses, symbols, plants, animals, mental concepts, angels, powers, magical images and much, much more. You will need to build up these lists if you are going to use planetary magic, or to direct your needs successfully. All these attributes act as a kind of telephone number, attracting the attention of a specific planetary force, which has the power to assist with a particular aspect of occult work, or mundane needs. Studying mythology, symbolism and the many layers of mystic correspondences forms a large part of any practical magician's training. Whether you tackle the vast array of material which is taught in Qabalistic schools or work from the Irish myths and Celtic legends to build up a data bank of material will depend on where your training is rooted; each system is valid and will produce results, but it does have to be learned and thoroughly understood before it will be helpful.

Magic works through symbols. If you show the inner a particular colour, number of candles, or the outline of a talisman you will be asking for a particular sort of response, which may well be given to you in symbols or colours or letters or the appearance of a certain animal in your dreams, but this will be meaningless and useless to you unless you understand what is being shown to you. It is rather like foreign language phrasebooks which give you the phonetic words for a particular question but do not show a similar explanation for the possible answers! Like mastering another language, magic requires study and practice, not the occasional dip into a tourist's phrasebook. Until you have mastered the basic elements of magical techniques any answers you get may be incomprehensible to you. It is for this reason that the exercises in the earlier part of this book are aimed at teaching you to make the important shift of consciousness into a state wherein magical reality can manifest and explain itself.

Each aspect of the basic exercises helps to train your inner occult muscles, and open up deeper levels of your psychic awareness. This works in two main directions. One allows you to focus very exactly upon one subject, setting aside all mundane concerns, and the second allows a much deeper awareness and understanding to bring forth clear answers to questions, or insights into symbols. You will gain what are called 'realisations'; that is, certain ideas or concepts are 'made real', are understood fully and suddenly. Quite often, realisations are about quite minor matters. Links are suddenly formed between pieces of information which you may have had in your head for a long time yet the instant they are put together, a whole, much larger piece of the picture becomes clear. You often want to say, 'A-ha!' and a sort of 'click' is heard in your head. This may not happen every time you sit down to meditate or each time you perform a ritual, but gradually you will get to recognise these realisations when they do occur, and also the conditions in your physical and mental state which cause them to happen most often. Once this stage is mastered you will be able to gain great benefits from every meditation session, each inner journey will offer up valuable treasures and all your rituals will be more effective.

Until you are able to gain realisations from your meditations it is pointless going on to more elaborate or ritualistic practices, as whatever good they might do for you will be missed, simply because you don't know what you are looking for. Certainly begin to fill up your data bank with the mythology of your homeland, or any other which calls to you. Muse over the stories, retell them to your children, or friends, or silently as you go to sleep, relive them. Gradually these will also begin to unravel their sacred mysteries. Walk in the natural places, even if they are small, public parks, not the wild moors or the rare forests. Listen to the sounds of nature, the wind in the trees or grasses, the cries of birds, the sounds and calls of animals. Look closely at the bark, the shape, the structure of trees so that you will recognise them in winter, or discover them in visions. There are many traditional secrets concealed in the names and natures of trees, yet they can be understood with patience.

Study books too, so that the words and interpretations of others, the pictures they have painted of ancient civilisations, of distant places and untamed regions fill your inner perceptions, to be recalled at need. Do not take anyone else's word as 'gospel', at least, not for yourself. Experience is the true teacher of magic, nothing else will have the same value. Certainly accept those ideas which have been received in dream or vision, or researched and interpreted from ancient sources as a starting point, but be willing to make your own discoveries, draw your own conclusions and experience your own revelations. Gradually you will find those illuminating flashes of realisation and deep understanding became more frequent, and their coming can be predicted by the way you approach each question. Knowledge will begin to flow to you, and in that is the seed of wisdom.

MAGICAL EQUIPMENT

You will need to gather around you a number of physical objects which will assist you with magical work. Recognise that such things have power because you give it to them, they do not have any inherent energy. A wand is just a stick until you bless it and fill it with magic. If you wave it about recklessly or show it to your friends it will revert to being a stick. Even if you are given something by another practitioner it will need to be attuned to your patterns, dedicated to your needs, and will not immediately bend to your will and solve all your problems. The same applies to things you might buy; each is a thing which is new to you and has to be focused to your use. Don't be led to think otherwise.

You will need a chair to sit on, and for those who have very limited means or whose families are extremely hostile, that may be as far as you can go. The next item is a table, cupboard, shelf or top of some fitting which can become an altar. The altar is a workbench, a display cabinet, a resting place of the Light of Creation, and many more things. It will need to be dressed with coloured cloths, candles, instruments of magic, systems of divination, symbols, flowers and all kinds of other things as your work progresses. You will find that inspiration will guide you to just the right things for each occasion, so be prepared to hunt through cupboards, visit sales or explore junk shops for the correct item for a particular piece of work.

You should have some sort of magical garment to put on, as you take upon yourself the image of the highest being within you. A

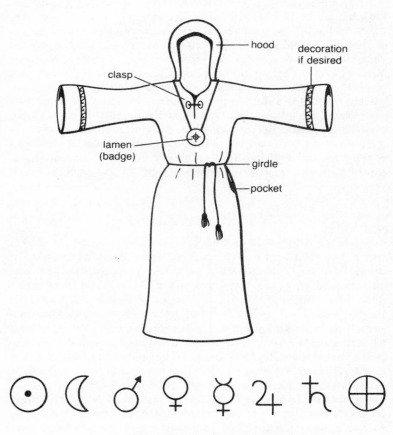

Robe and Planets decoration

proper magical robe is made of a natural fibre, silk, cotton, linen, wool or a mix of these, and is usually ankle-length, long sleeved, with the opening at the neck closed with a brooch or symbol. It can be any colour and pretty well any shape. The simple 'T' shape involves only two seams of sewing, from wrist to armpit to hem on each side. There is no shaping necessary, and the garment should be loose enough to get in and out of easily. Normally it is worn over a clean, naked body, for real ritual, but circumstances may make it necessary to be worn over some clothes, so leave room. It is not intended to be expensive nor a fashion item. Embroidery or other decoration is up to you. For out-of-doors rites a simple cloak, made of something like knitted jersey material, gathered on to a cord at the neck for tying, with a hood of double material sewn on, is very useful. Books on stage costume or children's fancy dress will give you lots of ideas. A length of coloured cord to go round your middle and some comfortable slippers or sandals complete the outfit for most workings. Even the sandals are not important, as having your bare feet on the ground or at least the floor can be a very earthing experience for the normally shod individual.

You will need containers for the elements as discussed in the last chapter, a platter to place the bread on and a cup for the communion. You will need an incense burner, which can be a terracotta flowerpot almost filled with clean sand, cheap enough from any garden centre. (Do remember to stick something over the hole in the bottom if you intend to carry incense around, otherwise you will mark your travels with a stream of sand and hot charcoal!) Try out different sorts of incenses, placed on lighted charcoal tablets until you find one you and your companions can enjoy. Some make folk sneeze or cough, or make their eyes water, so be careful. You will need a supply of candles and safe holders for these. Ordinary white candles are fine but coloured ones may be used to harmonise with the purpose of the rite, or represent the elements at the Quarters, for instance.

You will need several books in which to write the results of your divinations and meditations, even if you record these on tape at the time. The concepts should be regularly distilled and written down in a form which can be consulted and referred back to – trying to locate a taped item takes far longer. You will also need a book to record the words and aims of your rituals. These need not be exact scripts, although a written text is easier to follow for beginners. However, reading from a script and rustling through the pages can break the concentration of the best ritualist, and ought to be avoided if possible. This means a regular ritual's words have to be learned by heart, and more elaborate ones have a framework of learned invocations, movements and so on, within which there is room for inspiration, silence or a predetermined pathworking, for example. It is important to record details of your ritual work, its objective, who took part, where and when it occurred and so on, so that in the future you can look back and see how well your spells have worked out.

There are lots of little things which you will have to collect as you progress, like the obvious boxes of matches, candles and tapers, charcoal blocks and various sorts of incense resins, sticks or perfumed oils and their burners. A temple corkscrew is useful for opening ceremonial drinks, as well as various small dishes for holy oils, libations or other loose objects to be consecrated. You might start to collect Tarot cards, divination systems, a crystal ball or black mirror for scrying (crystal gazing) rituals involving knowledge of the future. You might require a sound system to play tapes or records during ceremonies, or pre-recorded pathworkings for your own meditations. Collect jars to keep incense grains in, clearly marked with the contents, and a biscuit tin for the cakes or bread will also come in handy. You might look out for a poster or make your own drawing of a symbolic scene for each of the elements, to be hung on the appropriate walls. You might make an elemental banner, appliqued cloth or painted on hardboard, if you have the inspiration.

The type of equipment and regalia you collect and make use of will depend a great deal on the kinds of rituals you intend to practise. It may depend on your circumstances, whether you have a room which can be set aside for ceremonial working which can be filled with magical symbols, or if you prefer the outdoor, basic rites of natural magic, using only the stones, twigs and seashells which you might find there. It may depend on your artistic abilities to some extent, although if you are willing to be inspired by the creative genii, you may discover all kinds of hidden talents, to carve, embroider, paint, write poetry or construct a valid magical atmosphere by thought processes alone.

In the end, it is the ability to create an atmosphere, a feeling of 'place and time' which is far more important than surrounding yourself with beautiful or expensive equipment. The most costly wand in the world, made by someone else, will be as much use to you as a wooden spoon from the kitchen drawer, and will have as much power. Take a simple rod, cut from a tree with care and forethought, hang it to dry for a couple of months, shape it, polish or varnish it, love it and handle it, and it will develop into a pleasing and effective tool in your hand in the way no bought item can do. Accept that it can become that which directs your will or purpose and it will do so, and it should be looked after carefully to retain its charge. If you sweep it in a circle about you, a line of sparkling fire will follow, which you will see once your psychic vision has been so trained. You will then have your basic circle, cleansed and made ready. That, for many kinds of rituals, will be enough. Later on you can all upon the elements and their guardians at the Quarters, seeing each as you describe it or invoke it to visible appearance. The elemental being does not appear because you are making it visible in the physical world. As you switch into your magical personality, you alter your level of awareness to take in some of the world of that other being's reality. You are raising your own rate of vibration, it would seem, so that you are able to perceive other realms of magical reality for yourself.

SETTING THE SCENE

Nearly all magical rituals take place in a physical space set aside and prepared for the ritual, into which is conjured another scenario, a historical setting like an ancient Egyptian temple, the Celtic wildwood, an Aztec pyramid or prehistoric stone circle. Many rites have their setting in 'otherworlds', perhaps the Underworld, realm of myths and legends; the Starry Temple set in the depths of space; or even an imagined setting beyond history or geography, some faerie land or sci-fi landscape. In each case the scene is carefully set, using powerful symbolic images, colours, shapes, God forms, architecture and ambience. Often this is done by a descriptive narrative, read or spoken by one of the participants, whilst all others sit with their eyes closed and mentally 'build' every detail, so that it becomes very vivid and real. You should not expect it to be visible in the same way when you open your eyes, however!

It is within the conjured vision of the other place that the power of the ritual will be invoked and contained, and from it will the energy be sent forth to begin its magical work. Only by being very aware of this double level of the magical place, accepting it and acting as if it is real, can you gradually learn to invoke, be aware of the power and direct it effectively. It is usually best, during all the parts of a ritual in which you are not actually speaking or moving, to remain quiet, with your eyes closed, reinforcing the setting, mentally echoing the words spoken by others, seeing the shafts of light which surround all the magical equipment and the patterns of energy which are clearly visible within the realm in which the mental temple is being constructed. This is another good reason why scripts and speeches should be kept to a minimum. The rustle of turning pages, especially if there are about ten people doing it, can absolutely destroy the concentration and focus of all, and so the vision of the inner temple will have no stability. Learn your parts, or make them up as you go along, within a pattern. Use gesture or mime and, above all, take it slowly, allowing symbols to coalesce fully on the screen of inner vision, so that you can feel them and interact with them.

To begin with, especially if you are working on your own, try to make the actual setting something like that which you intend to envision. Face a door, for example, if you are going to imagine a doorway to another world, or a window, if you can see some sky or the moon. These things will help make your inner vision clearer. Keep your first workings very simple. Imagine a natural scene, perhaps, which you will have in your memory of trips to the country, like a wood, a seashore or an ancient sacred site, rather than a complex Egyptian temple scene. Close your eyes and spend time building up the various parts of the setting you have chosen. Feel the wind, smell the leafmould, hear birds or animals moving in the undergrowth. Work at it until it does feel different from the normal atmosphere of your room. Always allow lots of time to make the change to the inner landscape, for that gently leads you into the right mental state in which you can work magic, see the future, discern the truth from divination and much more. The clearer and more real the images in your mind's eye, the greater will be your power to create changes in the future of your world, for healing one person or the whole planet; for gaining wisdom or understanding, and evolving yourself into a better person.

You must be aware that you are not 'inventing' what you see, but are calling up images from memory, from past lives, perhaps, and from the infinite store of material encapsulated in the Akashic Records, (which can be described as a universal astral databank). In these hidden resources all human memory is contained, from the first visions of prehistoric people, and maybe even views of the future. By learning to enter freely and perceive scenes invisible with your eyes open you will discover just how vast a store can be reached. When you come to 'create' a scene for a pathworking or the setting of a ritual, you are not making it up but, by carefully observing the symbol code, seeing a different part of reality. What is important to learn is the system of timeless symbols which have been handed down to us through the ages, recorded in the oral traditions of myth, legend, song and poem.

If you mix up bits of different traditions the result will be as upsetting as if you had mixed up the courses of a meal. No one would really enjoy soup mixed with salad mixed with apple pie and cheese, all stirred together. No magician will enjoy a ritual with bits of Celtic myth mixed with Egyptian God forms, swirled round with Tibetan chanting and Qabalistic colours! If you do not know enough, or are too idle to learn a matching set of symbols, colours and God forms, etc. you are far too idle to venture into magic, for you will come to harm that way. If you are not in a position to learn a wide variety of symbols of one or several traditions you will have to ask for help from the inner realms direct. By being sincere and respectful in your request for help, and having the sense to be still and listen to what is being told to you, you will get the help you need. You will still have to construct the setting for your ritual from what the inner powers show you, and act towards them in ways which acknowledge that they are real when you call upon them, but you will at least be shown corresponding symbols.

To build any scene requires patience and perseverence, so you must be observant of what things in your own world are like, and what their magical counterparts must be like. Start with a simple country scene, or a traditional temple. See the area in front of you, with your eyes closed. Look at the floor and see how trees or pillars meet it. Build upwards, a little at a time. Look at the walls, or the greenery of the forest. See it in detail, leaf by leaf, or stone by stone. Let it become real. Feel the atmosphere, the natural sounds. To begin with, concentrate only on what is before you, the furniture, the natural objects, and leave the calling down of God forms alone. Sink fully into the reality of the scene and then, keeping the vision fully in mind, open your eyes and perform all the stages of the ritual, the consecration of yourself, of the circle, and the magical sphere of focus and protection. When you close your eyes you should still be able to see clearly the scene you set before you began.

Gradually, with practice, you will be able to weave together the physical objects in your actual ceremonial space with their inner counterparts, and hold the double image clearly. When you are able to share your rituals with other people, some of them, as the rite progresses, will have the mental time and energy to maintain the setting whilst others interact with it. That is one of the main advantages of group work.

When you have had a fair amount of success with building the scenery you can allow the Gods and heroes to enter the scene. You cannot command them, they are bigger and older and wiser than you, but on the whole they are kindly, so will appear to you, to help with your magic, offer teaching or divinatory omens, if you give them time to speak. They are real. They are powerful and need to be treated with respect and politeness, even if they don't appear half as dramatic as you might like! They will appear to you in a muted form, so that you can recognise them from their costume, symbols or colours, not as they are in their own realm. They will speak inside your head, in your own language, if you are sensible. Only the stupid or very rash call upon Gods of War or Terror to appear, even if they do think these mighty beings can sort out their domestic affairs!

EXERCISE EIGHT – MEETING THE GODDESS

Prepare yourself as if you were going to meditate, with your chair, notebook and pen. Light some incense if you like it, and a candle or lamp. Sit very still and relax with your eyes closed.

Imagine as well as you can an arched stone doorway. See the way the blocks have been cut to fit the curve, the decoration on each side at about head height, the top of the pointed arch and its carved keystone. Feel the texture of the rock. Then focus on the fact that the arch is closed with a curtain of heavy, dark blue cloth, rather than a wooden door. Smell the material. Notice how it stirs in a hidden draught. See it start to flap, and then as if an invisible hand had lifted a corner, see it raised so that you can look beyond.

Discover the different textures of light and shade now becoming clear to you. Gradually allow your vision to settle upon the dark shape revealed against a brightly lighted hall. Notice how it takes form and becomes clearer. After a while you discover it is actually the figure of a woman, in a dark, hooded cloak which covers her as she sits on a high-backed chair. The light is shining in behind her through a clear window with many tiny, diamond-shaped panes of glass, set in lead. Gradually the colour of her cloak is revealed, again a deep blue, sprinkled with tiny flecks of silver.

She puts back the hood with pale, long-fingered hands and reveals a face of great beauty, surrounded by a cloud of dark auburn hair, falling in curling waves on each side of her face. Her eyes are deepest blue, and though her skin is pale, there is a blush of health on her cheeks, and she is smiling. As her cloak is pulled away from her shoulders, her gown is seen, pale and shimmering silver, over a dress of sea green. At her feet the carving on the chair is picked out in silver, too, revealing the crescent of a new moon.

In her lap is a vast and ancient book, bound in black leather, carved and embossed with silver and moonstones. Her voice, when she speaks, is soft and low, filled with the undertones of song. She says, 'This is the Book of Dreams, is there anything you would like to know?' Somehow, you find the courage to go towards her, and sit at her feet on a low stool, set close to the silver moon. You ask about your own dreams, your hopes and desires. She may tell you her name, she may offer a gift, or you may converse in words or silence, until you are answered. You see the great chair on which she is seated is built like the prow of an old-fashioned wooden boat, and a carved figurehead stands behind her. The wood is black and picked out with shimmering silver.

Eventually you know that it is time to leave, and you rise to your feet, thanking her for her advice or help. As you return to the curtained doorway she speaks out loud again: 'I am the Mistress of Time and Tides, I rule the wilds of sleep, my minions guard the cloudy rides, my books all secrets keep.' Then the curtain closes and darkness falls around you. Collecting your thoughts and visions and the answers you may have gleaned, you gently open your eyes.

As you will see, it is not necessary to envision a complex or complete temple. This visit to the Moon Goddess will offer much thought and help to you, especially with regard to your psychic powers, which are vital to your ability to envisage and build the temples and sacred places you will construct for your own work. Using an outdoor setting, discover a landscape for an encounter with the Sun God. See his symbols, his colours and his environment, and hear what he has to say about Light, and Life, and Liberty.

5 · THE POWER, THE PATTERN AND THE PURPOSE

It can be done. It is the art of Master Changer, and you will learn it, when
you are ready to learn it. But you must not change one thing, one pebble, one
grain of sand, until you know what good and evil will follow on that act. The
world is in balance, in Equilibrium. A wizard's power of Changing and of
Summoning can shake the balance of the world. It is dangerous, that power,
it is perilous. It must follow knowledge, and serve need. To light a candle is
to cast a shadow. . . .

A Wizard of Earthsea
Ursula Le Guin

All acts of magic need three things: power, a pattern and, most
important, a purpose. Power comes in a variety of forms; from that
which is in everyone as their life force, yet which can be focused and
manipulated so potently, to the great powers of the Creator of the
Universe, and of the Gods, Goddesses, angels and elemental beings.
By learning to raise and direct your personal power you will find that
this acts as a catalyst to those vast forces within the universe. If you can
control and direct your own inner stength and at the same time, ask for
assistance from some greater being, it is amazing what can be achieved.

The hardest part is learning control over your own will, being able to be exact and precise as to what you want, and seeking it in the most effective way. Often that objective can quite easily be achieved by sheer hard work, by study or some quite ordinary method. What needs to be understood is that magical methods should only be applied when every possible mundane avenue of gaining what you need has been fully explored. Magic is not a short cut, nor will it reward you nor fulfil your greed. Magicians *can* change the world. Their carefully considered aims, which are for the benefit of all humanity, can be made concrete. Many improvements have been made, especially recently, in world affairs, because magicians of good will have sought such changes, but these are the experts, working in conscious harmony with the Divine Plan, not wary novices seeking change for its own sake.

THE POWER

It is through the often apparently boring activities of meditation and inner journeying that you begin to understand the nature of the powers, Gods and heroes, so that you know instinctively who to ask for what sort of help. You understand the way you can gain their attention, the kind of offering, of incense or flowers, or your own effort, which will bring your needs to their consideration. Nothing will buy their help; you cannot bribe the Gods nor can you order them to obey or command them, but by asking politely, by using the symbolic 'telephone number' of correspondences you can make your request known, and if it is just, you will be helped.

The Gods and elemental beings are totally real and the only difference between us and them, apart from age, size, power and temperament, is that their dwellings are in different 'dimensions', for the sake of argument. They can be encountered if we make the conscious journey to their realms and, by invitation, they can affect things which happen in the future of our dimension of the time/space continuum. If we want their help we must visit the places where they are to be found. Some of these have natural equivalents on Earth. For example, if you wish to meet an Undine, the elemental of Water, go to the sea, a lake or clean river, switch into a passive mode, and your chances of meeting an Undine are greatly increased. The same applies to the Dryads of the woods, or the Gnomes of the rocky places, caves and mines. The ancient Gods and Goddesses of Egypt or Classical Greece are slightly more difficult, as they are not likely to be encountered in Croydon or Illinois unless they have been brought there by someone who knows how to recreate their natural temples and Olympic homes in those places.

If you ask for help from some mighty being, you may well get that help, but you probably won't see the Goddess at work or the elementals improving your garden plants' health. Magic always looks like a coincidence. You are unlikely to discover archangels on your doorstep with your desire on a silken cushion, but you might discover the vital object in a junk shop or as a gift from a long-lost auntie! If you are precise and clear about your aim and you have the sense not to try to dictate to the inner realms how they should accomplish this, you stand a fair chance of getting what you ask for. Many people make the mistake of trying to plan out the steps by which some objective might be reached, and that will break the spell so that it fails. You must have one request in mind, something which you must have tried to obtain by other means first, and that thing must be an 'end result', that is, not 'money to go on holiday with ' or 'a legacy to buy a house', but the need for the holiday or the house. Money, being only one link in a chain, is not something that can magically appear, but whatever it is needed for can often be attained if the right sort of request is made.

You need to realise that the whole world is an organic, living system. Because it is alive it is subject to change – magic is understanding and controlling changes, so a magical ritual will seek out that node in the natural pattern of changes and fit your request in. For example, if you need a particular rare book, the angels will not conjure it out of the air in front of you but will make you aware of a secondhand book shop where it happens to be for sale, or, on a particularly good day, that rare book might turn up discarded in a skip of rubbish cleared from a house, or as a gift from a friend! Someone else has got rid of the book and now it is your turn to have it. The same applies to everything to which magic might be applied, from finding a parking space to feeding the starving in Bangladesh. There will be someone moving out of the spot you need for your car 'coincidentally' at the moment you arrive. There is enough food in the world at any time but most of it is in the rich West, not the destitute areas. Magic can help make the connections which, in time, will lead to the transportation and sharing of those surplus requirements.

By learning to raise your own 'puny' personal power you can use it to plug into a vast and potent source of magical energy, so that gradually you will gain greater control, and be able to tackle greater projects. Again, there are no short cuts except continuous effort, to refine your will, to understand need and greed, to look at long-term outcomes and objectives. Change will come, sometimes very slowly. An effective spell can take years to work, although many work instantly; the speed depends on the scale of the change needed. Also, you have to consider long-term effects which might result from your immediate request. We are all living in a dynamic system so that a change in one part will minutely affect all the rest. This is the principle by which astrology works – the planets are relatively small and far away, but their continual motion in relation to each of us can have a distinct and tangible effect. The slight movement of Saturn from one configuration to another in our horoscopes and lives can be profound and significant! The same applies to magic. One small spell can set in motion a chain reaction which can alter our entire world.

At the start of nearly everyone's magical activities, changes in their lives seem to happen with great rapidity and usually cause considerable disruption and confusion. This is not the result of calling up demons, merely a demonstration that they are dealing with real forces of change, and these are not being controlled by the novice. This force of change will follow a magician throughout his entire career, often helping by showing opportunities, and sometimes seeming to hinder by causing a sudden break-up of familiar patterns. However, when the upheavals are over the new pattern is always better than that previously experienced. You have to learn to trust and hang on when the waters of the inner are stirred by some kind of storm, and accept that a safe harbour will be reached.

Strange as it may seem, those people who take up the practices of magic at a mature age, say 25-plus, often make much faster progress than their younger, and much less experienced, though definitely more enchanted, associates. If you have been through all the changes of holding down a job, making a family home, caring for children and gaining the millions of priceless experiences which life can throw at you, those upheavals which magical training can cause will be weathered far better. It is important to have a stable base, and occult knowledge is no substitute for the basic foundation of home, job and family. Nor will magic fill any gaps in your life without a great deal of hard work. If you don't have a job, magic may help you find one, but you might not like it. If you have no love in your life, magic will not supply it, until you learn why you are not lovable, and that can be a very hard lesson. Learn to love yourself, respect others and gradually you may find the gaps in your relationships fill with warm and lasting friendships. Occult abilities can make your life easier, but you have to

61

learn the difficult occult skills first, and trust your new-found visions and intuition.

The inner beings that cause these upheavals in your life are not cruel; they may seem careless towards such fragile beings as ourselves, but they wish to work hand-in-hand for the accomplishment of the evolution of the universe. Problems arise in the areas of misunderstanding between us and them. We cannot see further ahead than the next few weeks in any detail, yet the beings who live beyond our timescale can see the way things are intended to go for the ultimate best results. We must learn that our actions may have long-term results and that what we begin as a simple act of magic may have far-reaching effects.

For example, we may be prompted to do some healing. A friend may have been injured in a road accident but, by our determination, makes a fast and complete recovery, gets back in a car and injures someone else. If that person had been left to the healing powers of medical science and time, he might have remained in his hospital bed, learning the lesson of careful driving and reflecting on the meaning and value of a healthy life. The other injured person might have been able to bring up her children to become great workers for peace or law, yet the accident she was involved in robbed her of that opportunity. Always, in cases of healing, ask that the right sort of healing be applied, not an instant, miraculous cure.

Every magician is responsible for the outcome of his rite. Whether it works out and gives him exactly what he expected (it doesn't very often, you get what is actually needed!) or some other outcome transpires, that result and its long-term effects are still his personal responsibility. This should be reason enough to think very hard about intervening by magical means in anything! Life is like a chess game; each move gives rise to other possibilities, and prevents certain other things from happening. It is no use thinking only of an immediate outcome; you must consider some of the future changes which may result from your present action. Ignorance is no defence. In esoteric terms, you are responsible and will remain so, until that chain of events is concluded.

You are also responsible for the people whose lives your magic affects, whether you initiate them into a lodge, heal them, or give them a simple Tarot reading. Each of these small events could alter their entire future paths through life, so do consider very carefully what you are doing, and what effects it might have for the future. People do take note of divinations, and act upon them. Initiation can

THE POWER, THE PATTERN AND THE PURPOSE

be a radical change, opening up aspects of a person's hidden talents for good, or desire for power over others. It should never be rushed, either when you are the candidate or if you are helping initiate someone else. There should always be time for reflection and consideration before such a major change.

When you wish to work with the various ancient sets of Gods and Goddesses you will have to really understand their natures and powers. It isn't really good enough to have read a book on the subject, you have to delve more deeply. If you don't know who is responsible for what sort of activity when you call upon them you may well be asking a God of War to sort out your health, or a Moon Goddess to increase your finances. There have been some really useful books written recently by Murry Hope on the Gods of Egypt, and of Classical Greece, and of the ancient Celts. These are by no means comprehensive, but they do explain something about the natures of various deities, how they may be approached, and what they can help with. Only by really immersing yourself in one tradition until you thoroughly understand it can you feel secure in calling upon those deities to help you. It doesn't much matter which tradition you choose, so long as you are willing to discover all you can about the tasks, symbols, powers, colours and abilities with which each mighty being is associated, their interrelationships, legends and sacred places. All these factors will have to be woven into the pattern of your ritual if you expect practical help, guidance or teaching from them.

THE PATTERN

The pattern of rituals is one of the few standard aspects of this very complex and varied subject. Although some rites may be extremely simple and be largely carried out inside your head, whereas others may involve many people, lots of equipment, fabulous robes and sonorous invocations, each will follow a similar set of stages. Obviously you will be wise to begin with the fairly basic pattern, learning step by step, and building your physical and mental stamina, your collection of regalia and equipment, and your ability to enter the inner realm of magic.

Every single rite begins with many stages of preparation. You need to select the precise purpose of the ritual, prepare any symbols, determine numbers of candles, colours of altar cloths, talismans, speeches, chants, inner journeys, music, regalia, communion bread, salt and wine, and much more. If there are several of you participating in the working, you will have to be in total agreement as to the aim and activities of the rite. This should always be a single objective, to begin with. Later on you can set up the circle and then use it for a healing rite, a divination and some sort of inner quest, but that is for those with a fair bit of experience.

A ritual pattern is formed on several levels. On the physical plane, you have to create the circular space, ideally with an altar in the centre and seats at the points of the compass for those participating. If you are on your own, working in a small space, you will have to be able to imagine your magical circle passing through furniture and, perhaps, walls.

You will need a period of time of about an hour minimum for a simple rite, to three or four for anything major. The ritual itself need not take that long to perform, but the preparation can take much longer than you think, especially if there are lots of items to be collected and made ready. You need time to become calm and set aside the worries of the mundane world, to take a bath or shower and dress in your magical robes.

You will then have to adopt your magical personality, and set out all the candles and symbols you are going to use. Later these will be blessed, the circle cast, the purpose of the rite stated, meditations and moments of silence to receive guidance woven into the pattern. There may be a time of activity, chanting, dancing, talisman making, divination casting, inner receptivity, or practical work in some other fashion to be arranged.

Then there should be a pause for thought before closing the circle, which generally starts with a communion, prayers of thanksgiving, for peace and other magnanimous ideals. This is followed by the final winding down of power, closing of each quarter, snuffing of candles, writing of reports and then the general clearing up and putting away of magical equipment, disrobing, and an earthing snack or hot drink!

These twelve or so stages need to be studied individually. Perhaps you will need to discover or write prayers to say as you bathe, so that you arise cleansed in body and spirit. You might use robing prayers to help you adjust into your magical personality, as does any priest as he vests before a service. Each item of magical regalia has a meaning and power and this should be acknowledged as you put it on. You will need to bless the Quarters and maybe light a candle, calling upon whichever set of Gods or angels you are working with to guard, guide and enlighten your magic. You may use each of the elemental instruments to circle the space with, saying a blessing as you go, or merely bow to each direction from your seat before the altar, if you have very little room. It will depend a lot on how simple or elaborate you wish to be, and whether or not you have any companions.

Next you should have the building of the temple, the narrative which outlines the setting on the inner levels of the ritual. Again this may be a very brief description of one aspect of such a sacred place, or a lengthy, detailed and complete conjuration of an entire scene. You will then need to pause for a few moments at least, to allow that picture to become real and visible with your eyes closed.

Next is the statement of the purpose of the ritual, which will be discussed in the next section of this chapter. It has to be a clear and precise request, or outline of a festival, or a thanksgiving, or divination, for example, and all present should have agreed with the purpose and be willing to add their energy to its accomplishment. This section is likely to be the longest, for it may contain mime, poetic speeches, dance, chanting, music, a further inner journey, or the setting up of a horoscope. At the completion of that section, it will again be necessary to pause, collect your thoughts and listen silently so that any inner guidance, answers to your requests or further inspiration can come through. (Even a firm 'No, you have asked for the wrong thing' can be heard occasionally.)

After that pause, any subsidiary work may be set out, although for novices it is far better to do only one thing at a ritual because it is extremely hard to maintain the level of concentration needed without several years' constant practice.

The first part of the closing is the communion, which is not any kind of insult to Christianity but an extremely ancient aspect of worship and shared ritual, whereby each participant acknowledges his divine origin and his unity with all beings, seen and unseen. By sharing the bread and wine all working groups are united, even if this is a momentary experience! They are also linked to all other people who celebrate a similar ritual, throughout time and space. It can be a truly uplifting moment, and again, should not be rushed. It may take some effort to be willing to take into both your hands the cup of shared drink, and in that moment look into the eyes of the giver, but it is an important magical moment. As you pass on the cup to the next person, he or she may equally find it hard to meet your gaze, which should be warm and loving.

After the communion is completed there should be another moment of quiet, so that the energies within the circle can gently begin to dissipate. Often there is a kind of business meeting, discussing future plans, work which has brought results, the raising of candidates through degrees, or names and details of future candidates. Sometimes stories are told, or instruction about the meaning of a festival is given, but these things really apply more to established groups with more than five members. However, you might find, even working alone, that you feel the presence of the Gods so strongly that they will talk to you, or give instruction or inspiration.

Finally it is necessary to close each Quarter in turn, in the reverse direction to that in which you opened, snuffing each Quarter light as you do so. The central light on the altar is usually left alight, and incense should also be allowed to burn out, unless its hot embers can be safely cast out onto the earth. Later on, the dregs of wine and bread crumbs should always be cast out to Nature. The closing should be slow and steady, and any residual power sent back into the Universe, to be reused later on. Any divine beings, Gods, angels or elementals whose presence you have invited should be thanked and allowed, of their own volition, to withdraw from your sight. You cannot command them to appear, nor can you order them to leave. You are the invader, travelling in your mind into their realms, so it is in fact your vision that retreats to its own normal awareness!

You will still have the tasks of clearing up, taking off your robes and putting away your instruments, and then making all the written records which are a vital part of practical magic. Only when you close the book and drink your cup of tea is the ritual really complete. If you have not felt great surges of power, or been made to see strange and mighty beings, it is probably because your magic is working properly! The more gentle the effects, the more powerful. If the ritual is well prepared, serious and runs smoothly, then it is far more likely to succeed than one in which you feel as if you are in a run-away rollercoaster, with strange visions rising from the incense smoke, and an overwhelming sensation of panic and disquiet.

You may well see things in your dreams, and discover the answers to your prayers in books, or the words of a friend, in the days to come, for that is how your ritual will fulfil its purpose. You should also feel fit and full of energy at the end, rather than exhausted and flat. The energy that every ritual raises ought to be controlled and some of it used to replenish the energy you use in the work. You should never feel drained, because, if you do, you are blocking the flow of power, and this can harm your health. The best way to ensure that no energy is lost is to go more slowly, allowing the power to rise, coalesce and then diminish gently, refreshing all those participating as well as accomplishing your ritual purpose. Never, ever rush. That is the cause of far more failures in magic than any other single factor. You can hardly work a magical ritual too slowly!

Be patient when you have completed a ritual. Do it as well as you can, being aware all the time if changes are needed in mid-rite. Allow a few moments of meditation or silence in between each section. Let other participants have their say during the rite, if they are inspired to speak, or can see or perceive anything important. When it is all over, share your experiences, and then, if the work has been to accomplish something in the future, do the hardest thing, *forget all about it!* This is part of the magic. If you keep niggling at what you have tried to do, worrying about whether or not it will work, you will prevent it happening. Just let the subject drop, for at least two weeks, preferably a whole month; by then there might be some results. If ideas pop into your head as a result of the ritual, note them in your book, but don't keep fretting about what you have done. It *is* done, and that is the end of it. A seed has been planted in another dimension and, just like a seed in the earth, it needs time to grow and materialise. Suddenly you will discover that what you asked for or something very like it, has appeared in your life. Then say 'Thank you!'

GIVING THANKS

When your ritual has been successful it is always worth having a small working of thanks, or including this as part of the next ritual. Burn some incense or set out flowers as you acknowledge what you have received. You may have a prayer for this, or simply, silently, from your heart, be grateful. Only by offering such thanks will you get your next request granted. The inner is full of potency for beneficial change, and the beings there will help, but you must, always treat them with respect, honour and thank them as best you can when something comes to a successful completion. Even if after several weeks, nothing seems to have happened, if you examine the area of your life about which you requested help, you will often discover that there has been a change, so gentle, so subtle that it wasn't noticed until you looked for such improvement. You must still say thanks, even if what you think you have received isn't quite what you asked for. That is the way of magic. It is surprising what you can be given, when you work for it, but you must always be aware that it might be what you need, not what you wished for!

Giving thanks is just one of the many forms of ritual you might wish to perform, design or discover. You will see from the above section that there is a variety of steps which nearly all rituals include. If you make a list of these you will begin to see what sort of task lies ahead of you, if you wish to become a ritual magician. You do have to create individual rites for yourself and your companions, for simply copying the words and actions of others will have little effect, and may well be quite different from what you actually need. This is why this isn't simply a book of spells – they just wouldn't work for you because your needs, abilities and experiences are different from mine. This is true of most books on magic. The rituals were written for other people in other circumstances, and though you may gain useful ideas, individual prayers or actions, it is really much better that you write or create your own sets, within the framework outlined above.

EXERCISE NINE – THE PATTERN OF RITUAL

Go through the earlier part of this chapter with a notebook and pen. On about twelve separate pieces of paper, write the numbers one to twelve, and then enter all that you can find out about each of the main sections of ritual, its preparation to the final clearing up. You will need to discuss these sections with your companions, or meditate upon each in turn, to discover how important it is to you.

You can also begin to enter such things as the equipment each section needs – for example, when setting out the Quarters, you will need four candles, candleholders and a box of matches. You might also need a pentacle, cup, wand and sword, four tables with different coloured cloths to put on them and four chairs for the Quarter officers to sit on. You will need an incense burner, charcoal blocks, and various sorts of gums and resins and herbs, and lots more. You may not wish to use all these things to begin with but it is as well to understand each thoroughly in case an opportunity arises in which you can share your work, or join a group of some sort. Go through all twelve (or more) stages and write out what you might need, what you already have, and what things you can make, buy or imagine.

THE PURPOSE

The purposes of ritual fall into a number of different types. You have seasonal festivals which form a very important part of the religious life of pagans and witches, for their arts are based around the story of their Goddesses and Gods. You may also celebrate your own festivals, birthdays, weddings, anniversaries, baptisms and funeral rites. You might enjoy marking the phases of the Moon, either new or full, the solar solstices and equinoxes, or even when the sun enters each sign of the zodiac, if you are interested in astrology. The main impulse of all the seasonal festivals in one of worship and interaction with the cycles of Nature, rather than constructive magic, although working with moon phases can enhance the effectiveness of your rituals for healing and psychic power, for example.

Another kind of ritual work is that of a formal lodge, which will have regular meetings to a set pattern, initiation ceremonies and probably rites through which suitable candidates are raised through a series of degrees as their knowledge and power increases. Witches also have initiation rituals, and some covens work a system of two or three degrees, as well as their seasonal and lunar gatherings.

Obviously you will have to be initiated into an established lodge, adhere to their system of training and symbolism and maintain their level of secrecy. Magical lodges are usually run as meritocracies rather than democratically. Your rise through the degrees will depend on your increasing abilities rather than on how long you have been a member, or how much money you can afford to put into lodge funds. In magic it is the skill to fulfil the position which matters, more often than not, so you may make fast progress or move up the ladder slowly. Only your own individual effort to gain skills, knowledge and practical experience will help you rise through the degrees, and if you have to spend years cleaning the temple silver while you gain knowledge from those above you, welcome that chance, as it is a rare honour! Given patience and lots of hard work you might rise to the point where you are the Lodge Master, in control of the training of green beginners with all the enthusiasm in the world, but not a clue as to how to work magic! What you learn as a novice will set the foundations of your whole magical career, so those foundations should be deep, strong and genuine or you won't get very far. However, real lodges and orders are fairly rare, and if you discover one and have the honour of being admitted to it, you should be very grateful.

Many of the rituals which individuals work are for self-awareness and inner guidance, or self-healing, or as a way of focusing their divinatory powers. These can vary from asking for help from the ancestors as shamans do, with drumming and dancing, to encountering a totem animal or tree, or Holy Guardian Angel who can teach the inner mysteries. You might wish to have an offertory ritual, to

69

give thanks for the success of a piece of magic, or when you offer yourself in dedication to a particular path, or even a self-initiation. You might need to perform a ritual for protection, cleansing or banishing unwanted habits or ideas, or to bless and protect a new house or even a new car.

Some rituals are public, performed as dances, mumming plays or sacred dramas, like the Mystery Plays which show the Biblical texts in an easily understood form to the ordinary people, yet also contain the mysteries of the various semi-magical Craft guilds. Ceremonies like Well-Dressing, the Abbots Bromley Horn Dance, the 'Obby 'Oss festival at Padstow in Cornwall, and the Helston Furry Dance, the Lewes bonfire celebrations and cheese rolling in Gloucestershire all preserve half-forgotten fragments of pre-Christian feasts and rituals. Many are concerned with encouraging the power of the Sun which, after all, we still depend on. For example, the making of round yellow pancakes to be tossed in the air, the chasing of round yellow cheeses down steep hills, the throwing of a golden ball or hot new pennies, the lighting of bonfires on hilltops, each represents the heat and light and power of the Sun. Dressing in disguises, in green leaves, and decking the streets with flowers all reverence the growing of Mother Nature, the return of Spring, personified by the May Queen or the Green Man.

Some rituals are for one single, straightforward purpose, like the magical dedication of a talisman, or for the healing of an individual, who might even be present at the ritual. In each case it is best to open the circle in your normal way, and then either make the talisman and bless it, or ask that the Angel of Healing assist your companion (if he is not there in person, he may be represented by a letter requesting help or a photograph, perhaps). As mentioned before, you should not act unless you have been specifically asked to do so, and you must not demand a healing, or anything else. Whatever sorts of magical workings you perform, always give the Gods the final say in the outcome. They are far wiser and more farseeing than we can ever hope to be. Certainly, they will show what is the best action, but we have to sit down and listen in quiet moments of meditation, and be willing to be guided by their silent instructions.

The most productive rituals for novices to perform are those which enhance your understanding both of your own inner abilities and your relationship with the other realms of the magical universe. These can take the form of pathworkings, where you re-enter past aspects of your current life and the relationships therein, to see them in a new and clearer light, or you can use a divination system. By carefully and ceremonially setting up the circle or temple, if circumstances permit, you will gain confidence and practice, so that these ritual actions become second nature and work effectively every time. This will lead to the gentle transition into those relaxed states of consciousness in which the reality of the inner realms makes itself clear. Once that happens it is much easier to get effective results from reading the Tarot cards or questioning the I Ching for guidance, or even scrying with a crystal ball or black mirror.

You can also set out to meet the Gods and Goddesses with whom you wish to work, in exactly the same way. Set up your circle and include a picture, statue or symbol which relates to their natural habitat; for example, a postcard of Mount Olympus for the Greek pantheon, a pyramid for Egyptian gods, or the branch of a particular tree to welcome our local Celtic deities. It doesn't have to be elaborate. Then read the stories of their lives and acts, or burn their incenses, play the music associated with their cultures, act out their legends, and then listen. Be still, wait in anticipation, and allow them to appear to your inner eye, to speak in the silence of your inner ear, to teach through direct knowledge which will flow through your attentive brain. Then say, 'Thank you' and offer more sweet scents, dance, song, poetry or whatever enters your head as being right.

Be willing to do lots of research. There are many excellent books, both old and new, which detail the stories, the landscapes, the sacred images of all pantheons, readily available in bookshop or library. Do your homework, create small collages of symbols, colours, illustrations and magical objects which you will learn are associated with your chosen deities. Embroider altar cloths, or make banners or wall hangings to decorate the place where you work and meditate. These can easily be rolled up out of the way when not in use, and they provide a fast and effective link to those powers from whom you seek aid. Experiment, always being cautious, polite and unhurried in your approaches, and you will be amazed at how strong, how appropriate and how immediate their help can be.

6 · RITUAL TRADITIONS IN THE WEST

We begin our journey in the temenos of the Mystery Schools, where we see how the Native Tradition flows into the Hermetic Tradition, and how these traditions have been preserved and fostered from ancient times up to our own. . . . We see how the role of the magician is a continuation of both shaman and mystery-priest . . .

The Western Way, Vol.2
John and Caitlin Matthews

Today we are not only faced with the choice of taking up or ignoring the magical opportunities which we encounter, but also of choosing from the wide selection of different traditions on offer. To a certain extent, what each student of the Mysteries does will depend on what guided him onto the paths of magic in the first place, or what kind of group his f.iends belong to, but it is important to recognise that we all have the right to choose. Although most people who search for truth through occult study change direction several times in their quest, life is much easier if the difficult choice of whether to stay with a group which no longer fulfils your individual needs, or to try for a different one, doesn't have to be faced too often.

In many cases, the student has no option as to which school he aligns himself with, because that is the only one in his area, or the first one he has had any contact with. However, there are now far more books written to guide novices, and many more short courses, systems of postal tuition and training schools for witches and occultists on offer. Any investigative student of magic will come across the references to these 'outer courts' fairly early in his reading, so he ought to know a little about the options before he can make the best choice.

Historically, there have always been secret gatherings of like-minded souls who have sought to learn more about the hidden or spiritual aspects of the world they found themselves in. Some of these schools have flourished within the established churches, blending mysticism with orthodoxy, and when their studies strayed too far from the straight and accepted path, keeping their work very quiet, in monasteries and secluded orders. In pagan times there were many such secret priesthoods, not merely worshipping their various deities but studying their powers, researching the sciences of the mind, the technologies of the intuition. Nearly all ancient wisdom traditions have left hints and clues about their even earlier foundations, about the way ancient knowledge was transmitted from elsewhere, across the sea, or from the deeps of space, carried to Earth by the light of the stars.

ATLANTIS

The oldest tradition is centred around the culture and magic of Atlantis, that legendary archipelago lost under the Atlantic Ocean. The legend tells that some natural disaster, or the perversion of magical knowledge, caused a cataclysm, shattering the mountains, sinking the islands and scattering their peoples across the seas. We do not know that this happened, nor can we prove that that first advanced civilisation, with its white cities, great temples, sacred colleges and scientific research establishments, was actually part of this material reality, yet most magical schools today give credence to the story and draw part of their heritage from those long-lost lands. Through the tunnels of time those who have been properly trained have passed back to that age before historic time and clearly seen the buildings, met the people, listened to the teachers, explored the arcane knowledge of star and land, of power places and inner skills.

The great temples' doors are no longer closed to those people who were their servants long ago. Many of the initiates seem to be alive now, at the end of the twentieth century, and through their modern magical training are able to recall or reawaken links with this foundation of our sacred heritage. Such work is one of the many tasks that students of the Mysteries are now being trained to undertake, so that the modern world may benefit more directly from the sources of ancient wisdom. Some such students are part of a group called 'The Atlanteans', a society founded in the West Country in the 1950s, and guided by the teachings of Helio Arcanophus. A few small groups continue this work today, but many other magical schools pay more than lip service to this ongoing fount of knowledge and power.

EGYPT

Another early tradition of magic and religion which has far clearer roots is that of ancient Egypt. From carvings, inscriptions, hiero-glyphic papyri and existing temples, a great deal of that heritage has come down to us.

The first thing that any students of this path must recognise is that they are dealing with a developing tradition spread over many thousands of years. What this means is that there are several distinct families of Gods and Goddesses, just as there were dynasties of pharaohs, and it is important to recognise which is related to which.

The most approachable, although not the oldest, is the pantheon based around the Goddess Isis, her brother/husband Osiris and their son, Horus. Also in this collection is the Goddess Nephthys, Isis' sister, married at first to Set, Osiris' dark brother, and then to the jackal-headed Anubis. Two other powerful deities of this pantheon are Thoth, the ibis-headed God of wisdom, and Hathor, cow-headed Goddess of motherhood and protection. You are certain to come across many other animal-headed deities who take part in the tangled story of the fight between growth and light, led by Osiris, and darkness and chaos, led by Set. You will also find different spellings of some of the names – Isis was actually rendered *Aset* in Egyptian letters, and Thoth was *Tahuti*. The cat-headed Goddess Bast is also called *Bastet*, and so on.

Working with the Egyptian pantheons is an interesting process, for despite the many thousands of years which separate their culture from ours, and the hundreds of miles from the Nile valley, it is still surprisingly easy to relate to these deities of the hot and sandy landscape. The first exercise which potential Egyptian magicians need to do is to discover for themselves exactly why Isis, whose

74

name actually means 'Throne', wears a vulture on her head, why Thoth has the head of a water bird, or why Sekhmet wears the face of a lioness. If you find a good illustration of your chosen God and Goddess, light a candle before it, or perhaps sit in the light of the sun, and quietly ask why, and then listen to the answer, the reason for these strange-seeming guises will be made clear to you.

GREECE

Another well documented and readily accessible tradition is that of Classical Greece. Here again, the legends of the Gods and Heroes, the battles in heaven and on earth, the dynasties of Gods and Goddesses have all come down to us, in sacred places, in carvings and in written texts. Details of the festivals and forms of worship are found on vase and wine cup in many a museum around the world. Excellent books, both learned and magical, reawaken this heritage of celebration and ancient wisdom, so that the sweet incenses to the Old Gods may burn on newly dedicated hearths, and the hero tales be re-enacted to bring forth their power. Their music lives on, the philosophies are still available to us, the writings may be studied in translation. The sacred sites of temples, theatres and healing sanctuaries may be visited, both on the mainland of Greece and her many islands which, like Atlantis before her, was a cradle of varied culture, religious observances and the birth places of the Gods.

You can picture Athene with her helmet and shield accompanied by her symbolic owl, sacred in many lands, standing in the white pillared temples on the heights of Athens, or wild-haired Hephaestus in his forge, creating in the fire the many artefacts of magic and power. You can approach mighty Zeus, father of the Gods, ruling Olympus; or moonlit Diana hunting with her bow in the woodlands, accompanied by her hounds; or Artemis, protector of women, Moon-mother; or dark Hecate who was worshipped in the light of the waning moon, at crossroads where her justice and revenge was sought and those daring enough asked for guidance from her ancient wisdom.

Among the Gods, the Heroes and the Fates there are plenty of characters to address your prayers to, or legends to enact to bring forth those qualities or powers into your own life or temple. Again, research and study, meditate upon a picture, sculpture or image of the places sacred to your deity, oracle or heroine. Ask for guidance as you taste the resinous wine, eat the mountain honey and burn the incense, Dittany of Crete, invoking with a pure heart and clear eye the ancient powers of Pan, the creator of panic, yet protector of animals and wild places. Try listening to the haunting strains of music played on the pan-pipes, and the other archaic instruments of Greece, recently recorded on convenient cassette or compact disc, and allow yourself to float back to the Hellenic hills, where naiads play and the great watchers in the cliffs above Delphi keep their timeless vigil over the sanctuary of light.

ROME

The Classical Roman world, although encroaching on our traditions in Britain, seems to have had less impact on the resurgence of pagan religion and magical practices. Wherever the Romans settled they became interested in the Gods of the place and, so as long as the natives accepted the idea that the current Emperor also had to be treated like a God, were happy to allow all kinds of religions to flourish. In the end, of course, this changed, because the Emperors were not always so god-like, and in many cultures no statues of deities were permitted. (Although the Celts carved magical heads they did not really personify their deities in the way the Romans did.) This was one of the reasons why the Roman army put down the Druids, and despoiled their sacred woodland groves, healing springs and ancient sanctuaries.

We are familiar with the names of the Roman Gods and Goddesses, some of them the same as the planets, those roving stars so important in astrology and magical arts. We are accustomed to Sol, Luna, Mercury, Mars, Jupiter, Venus and Saturn, and anyone who studies the practical art of talisman making, for example, must spend time setting out lists of the corresponding colours, numbers, metals, incenses, plants, animals, symbols and hours of the day dedicated to each. In this way their power is sharply focused when the talisman is charged and put into action.

Another aspect of the Roman influence, which may be encountered when you visit such places as the temple of Sulis Minerva at Bath, is that of a sacred place dedicated to both healing and divination. As at Delphi, recent research and archaeological explorations have revealed that there was an oracle attached to the sanctuary above Britain's only natural hot spring. Here priestesses would sit in the steamy atmosphere and utter prognostications about future events, the outcome of healing treatment and national and international happenings, to those waiting to hear. Also, in the great temple's courtyard were the altars of the Haruspex, the priest who would divine from the entrails of sacrificial birds or animals the future of the person who made the offering, or how successful the Emperor's campaign might be. He would also take note of the direction and number of birds flying across the sacred precincts, and of their calls, as a form of divination.

A system of ritual divination which has Roman roots is geomancy, which means 'earth divination'. In its simplest form the enquirer thinks of his question whilst prodding lines of dots into the earth or a sandy place. He makes four lines of any number of dots, without concentrating, and the diviner examines each line to see if the number of dots is odd or even. From this, a simple pattern of four lines of single or double dots is drawn out. There are sixteen possible combinations, each of which is a figure in the geomantic system, each having a precise lucky or unlucky meaning, an astrological interpretation and other significances which the diviner will explain. Each geomantic figure has a Latin name – *via* the way; *rubeus*, red; *populus*, the crowd, etc. – and by considering the complex interpretation of each figure in connection with the question, a favourable or unfavourable outcome may be predicted. This system has been largely overlooked in recent years but, like the runes, its power and complexity are being reassessed by modern magical diviners.

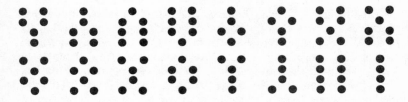

THE DRUIDS

At the same time as the Roman army was marching across Europe, the Celtic Druids were carrying out their teaching, healing and magical arts in the forested places of the wilderness. There were three sorts of magicians, usually lumped together under the heading of Druids. These were the Bards, the Ovates or Vates, and the Druid priests and priestesses themselves.

The Bards and Druids were initiated into the Mysteries of the West, taking many years to learn by heart the vast amounts of history, genealogies of the kings, poetic verses, laws of the land and the skills of healing, astrology and magic. These were the teachers, the keepers of records, the storytellers and the pagan priesthood, leading the ceremonies, giving divinations and making the offerings to their Gods and Goddesses. The Druids sought the sacred mistletoe, growing as it occasionally does on the ancient oak trees, from which their name may derive. The Bards sang the lays of the kings and heroes, brought news and information to the people, led them in their appreciation of the world beyond their villages and homelands. They would be inspired to create verses extolling the virtues of clan chiefs, telling of their deeds, their riches and their power. They maintained through memory alone great stores of knowledge, the lists of lineages, the deeds of long-dead heroes and many other verses, some of which ran on for hours, accompanied by harp music.

The Vates were much closer to the magical shamans of the West, drawing their power directly from their relationship with Nature. They were initiated directly by the Gods and Goddesses they communicated with, rather than by the Druidic hierarchy. In Christian times, they became the holy hermits, living alone in caves, giving forth wisdom, healing and guidance, and drawing on divine sources alone for their inspiration and skills. They would maintain the links with the ancestors, selecting the totem trees and animals, perhaps, for the children of the tribes, naming them and preserving the native wisdom which is sought by direct revelation, or mediumistically from those in the Otherworld. As the Bards traditionally wore blue and the Druids white, the Vates wore mainly green, linking them closely with their natural environment, from which they drew their herbal knowledge. They may have been associated with the siting of the sacred groves, the tree temples of the wild wherein the Druids met to teach, and celebrate their solar and lunar feasts. They may have recognised the lines of Earth power, the ley lines, and been able to imbue stones with vibrational energy, detectable among similar stones by those psychically aware to this day.

THE SAXONS

When the Saxons overcame the Romano-Celtic people, bringing their ploughs to the flat Eastern lands and their rune craft to the minds of the indigenous people, a new concept emerged. Originally the sets of rune signs were magical sigils, not letters of an alphabet as they became later on. Each one was named after a God or an event like dawn, which gave them either a protective power or a means of divination. Today there is a resurgence of interest in this intricate subject and sets of runes, presented as tiles or cards or wooden blocks, are appearing in the esoteric marketplace. These can be used for divination in a similar way to the Tarot cards; they can also be used for protection and as magical spells. By combining rune symbols occult messages can be spelled out, to frighten off thieves, to guard against fire, to bring wealth or a successful partnership in love or business. Like all systems, they need to be understood fully before their power can be harnessed to help you foresee the future, or defend your property against vandalism.

Not only are the Saxon runes becoming popular, but the many magical arts of these peoples are being rediscovered. There are early texts on the uses of herbs and plant magic, on spell weaving, and students of our Saxon and Norse inheritance are reviving the costumes and language. A totally invented system of wicca, or Saxon witchcraft, has even been published by Raymond Buckland. Mixing aspects of the reborn witch traditions of Britain with bits of worship of the old Norse Gods, a new ritual system has been offered to those who feel it could be their path. Other authors are working on magical uses of the runes alone, although patterns of ritual may be constructed around runic texts and useful spells.

THE MIDDLE AGES AND THE ENOCHIAN TRADITION

The islands of Britain were subject to many invasions of cultures, from the Norman Conquest to the years of the Crusades. There was always a far greater contact between peoples in Europe, in what is now France, Germany, Holland and much further away, through more trade and military exchange than many modern history lessons suggest. We in Britain share ancestors and traditions with much of Western Europe; our legends of King Arthur and the Holy Grail, for example, are to be found as far East as modern Iran. All through the Middle Ages bards and singers, master craftsmen and soldiers wandered right across to the Holy Land, and brought back facets of those different cultures, new foods, new herbs and new knowledge. From the region of the Arabian Desert came the ancient knowledge of astronomy and the star names we use to this day, Betelgeuse, Aldebaran, Spica, Sirius, Al Deneb and many more.

Also came the concept of 'zero' and with that the almost magical art of mathematics took on its modern form. In Queen Elizabeth I's reign, her advisor was the astrologer, mathematician and magician, Dr. John

Dee. He set the date for her coronation by studying her horoscope, and was known throughout the land for his wisdom and extensive practical skills. He helped to draw the maps with which Sir Walter Raleigh and other merchant venturers sailed across the Atlantic in seach of new lands. He and his associate, Edward Kelley, brought from a tomb in Glastonbury two magical powders and with them transmuted part of a copper warming pan to gold.

Dr. Dee, whose magical black scrying mirror and crystal ball can be seen in the British Museum, sought further knowledge from the angels themselves. Setting up a table on protective wax talismans, and sometimes using a young boy to scry or sometimes Kelley, Dee was shown a magical alphabet and a system of ritual evocation using a number of sonic calls, named the Enochian tradition of magic. It is a complicated and very powerful system and should never be played with, but modern magicians following in Dee's footsteps have learned more about the uses of the great talismans, squares of letters in the Enochian script, from which magical formulae may be obtained. Scholars have worked with the many messages and decoded parts of the Enochian language. Others, working again with scrying, or travelling in the spirit vision as it used to be called, have been shown similar inscriptions in the same strange alphabet, which they have been told was Atlantean. It is very mysterious but it is one of the traditions of magic which is being rediscovered at the end of the twentieth century, even though it was first made clear in the sixteenth.

ALCHEMY

Alchemy was also being more widely studied in Dee's time, and still today there are living and working alchemists, particularly in France. This is a multilevel system of study. It has links with chemistry and more recently, the atomic structure of all materials and the possibility of transmuting one metal or chemical element into another, which has parallels on a deeper, philosophical level too.

Dr. Carl Jung, a pioneer in the art of psychoanalysis, was fascinated by alchemical texts, and saw that part of the symbolism could easily be linked to the individual's quest for self-determination. The transmutation to pure gold could be applied to the human soul rather than metallic lead. The seeker for personal perfection could mirror the alchemical stages of dissolution, coagulation, blackening or distilling into pure substance in his own similar mental processes, the strange and unsettling changes which are so much a part of practical magical training. This is not a very common branch of magic, although the understanding of the importance of dreams, our relationships with deities, the ability of the mind to affect the body, our psychic faculties, and our use of symbols to express those experiences which go beyond words, all come within Jung's very wide circle of study.

MYSTICAL CHRISTIANITY

Underneath the scientific advances which magicians shared with the researchers there has been a stream of religious mysticism. The Celtic Christian Church was able to assimilate some of the teachings of the Druids, who worshipped a God called Esus, who died on a tree. The original church at Glastonbury, dedicated to Mary the Virgin, was supposedly built by Joseph of Arimathea in about 34AD, far earlier than any other proto-Christian edifice in Britain. The remains of the tiny wattle church, close to the ruins of the medieval church, were located by archaeologists, and there is plenty of evidence that the strange Tor rearing up from the level marshes was always a sacred place, from the Stone Age onwards. It was then, and still is, a centre of pilgrimage for Christians and pagans alike, for all have some religious connection with the old church, the newer church, or the sacred hill and its magical red spring in the valley. Joseph was there, the Holy Grail was there and perhaps, in the mists of Avalon, King Arthur and Merlin are there to this day, hidden only by a shift of dimension.

Within the Christian Church, in its long, tangled and often cruel history, many sects and even magical traditions have existed. From the holy hermits, dwelling alone in the wild places, the dedicated holy women who, in Celtic times, kept the sacred springs of healing water blessed and who cared for the sick, to the more recent dedication of many such special springs to Christian saints, a secret tradition has survived. It has survived, too, in folk celebrations, the ritual processions on Plough Monday, the pagan Yule log at the Christmas Feast, garlanded with pagan holly, ivy and magical mistletoe. It lives on in the May Day festivities, maypole dancing, the hobby horses which dance as human substitutes for the ancient animal sacrifice. Many churches still hold in their stoney arms the faces of the Green Man and the Moon and Earth Goddesses in the guise of cat or deer or flower. Many of their saints' days celebrate far older pagan ideas, from Lady Day in March, through St. John at Midsummer to Michaelmas at the autumnal equinox. Even Easter recalls the Goddess of Spring,

Eostre with her sacred hares and eggs and sprouting greenery far more blatantly than many Christians, if they thought about it, might like!

There have always been Christian Mysteries, such as the transubstantiation of the bread and wine at the mass, reflecting an earlier communion in which it was grain, the flesh of the Earth Goddess, that was eaten, and the blood of the God of the vine which was drunk in honour of those ever-living, ever-evolving deities. Within the monasteries and enclosed communities much wisdom, healing and spiritual power was hoarded, and the light that burned on many altars in ancient village churches kept alive a pagan flame, kindled on different altars long before. The Old and New Testaments provide much material for reflection, meditation and deep thought, just as any other historical/mythological texts do. Meditating on the words, the works and the magical acts of Jesus is just as valuable an occult exercise as looking only at pagan myths, or hero tales. No one says you have to accept any written source as gospel, unless to you it is, but because the influence of the Christian Church, for good or ill, has been so important in Britain and the West for many hundreds of years, it should not be ignored to suit a neo-pagan mind.

The pattern of the Church's feasts has kept alive the rites of Candlemas; St. Brigid took over from the earlier Goddesses of Spring, wells and healing. Lady Day in March celebrates the conception of the Star Child, born in a cave at Yuletide among the beasts of the field, as were many older Gods before him. Many saints, especially those in Cornwall and the far West, were pagan spirits or guardians of magical places. St. Ea who became St. Ives, St. Just in Roseland, St. Mawgan, St. Erth, St. Mewan and many more, each protected some sacred spot, with its standing stones, old before the Celts came, each with its healing well or shady grove. St. Mabyn, the hidden son of the Goddess Modron who is also celebrated at Madron's Well, St. Kew and St. Tudy and St. Issey, are all previous hermits or Goddesses. There are plenty more where those came from, and the legends of their magical deeds are being rediscovered all the time.

THE QABALAH

As well as the influence of the Saracens after the Crusades, other travellers from the East left traces of their beliefs, their philosophy and their magical arts. One of the strongest, which flourishes to this day, is the Qabalah. Originally a Jewish oral tradition, rather than a religion, it is based around the symbolic glyph of the Tree of Life. This is a depiction of ten interlinked circles, roughly in the shape of a tree, which represents the manifestation of various powers emanating from the Creator and coalescing into matter towards the bottom sphere, which is Malkuth, the Earth. Each of the ten spheres is associated with a planet or heavenly manifestation, and the pattern of spheres is linked by a series of paths. Each sphere has a magical image, used in meditation, as does every one of the twenty-two interlinking paths. It is from this glyph that the term 'pathworking' was derived. By clearly seeing in your mind's eye the symbolic image of the sphere from which you are commencing your inner journey and then mentally following the relevant path towards another sphere, you pass through a mental barrier which frees your inner vision to take in a great deal of magical information.

Each sphere is associated with an angel or archangel, and various powers, names, colours, God-forms and Hebrew titles of God, all of which form the basis of Qabalistic rituals. By learning and understanding who is represented where on the Tree, what such beings are to be called, which colours, numbers, incenses and symbols are relevant to that sphere, you have a firm foundation of talismanic magic, of personal growth through seeing where you stand on the paths, and of mythology. The Tree is also represented as standing in four worlds so there are, in fact, four sets of colours, names, powers and other correspondences. It is a vast and complex system, yet one of the most commonly used traditions in Western ritual magic.

The Hermetic Order of the Golden Dawn, founded at the end of the last century and still continuing in an evolved form in America or in small groups scattered around Britain, bases its ritual system of ten degrees on the pattern of the Tree. There are ten officers who occupy the positions of the spheres, from the newest initiate at the bottom to the Hierophant on his throne in the East, at the top of the Tree. The ritual system is very formal, the rites are wordy and, to today's magicians, quite archaic-sounding. Nevertheless it is a powerful system when worked sincerely, and from its enfeebled rootstock grew many of the modern magical orders and fraternities which meet in secret today. Dion Fortune was a member of one offshoot of the Golden Dawn, as was Crowley, and many other writers famed for revealing this arcane knowledge in publicly available books.

Don't expect to find such orders in the 'yellow pages' or obviously advertised in the esoteric press, although if you are diligent, you might encounter a lecture which leads to the 'outer court'. This is where new students are trained in the symbolism of Qabalah, its uses and meanings, the meditations and pathworkings which empower those following that system, the simple rituals which bless and protect, and the applications of the Tree of Life as a plan for right living. After this basic training, those who are deemed worthy may be invited to become members of one of the lodges of high magicians, and enter the sacred and secret portals of initiation. Then begins the long and arduous journey upward through the grades, some relating to the elements, some to the planets, and all reaching toward adepthood and personal perfection.

The Qabalah is often used as a solo system, as a basis for regular meditations and inner journeys. There are forms of Tarot divination associated with the Tree, fitting the Major Arcana on the paths and attributing the minor cards to the ten spheres in the four worlds. There are Qabalistic rituals of self-dedication, cleansing and protection, as well as ways of making talismans, performing rites for healing, becoming invisible, and all kinds of other things. On its long journey from the East to the Christianised West, the Qabalah has accreted to itself all sorts of mythologies, and many people use the pattern of the Tree as a kind of universal filing system, hanging the Norse Gods or the Celtic heroes from its branches, as they in turn hung from their own trees, or sought wisdom from the talking twigs of Celtic divination. Like any data system, many things can be fitted into the niches it provides, but not all traditions sit comfortably with it, and none should be forced into ten-fold division if it is designed for the lunar nine-fold pattern or the zodiacal twelve parts.

WITCHCRAFT

The other major development in the last thirty or so years is the resurgence, or some would say the total reinvention, of witchcraft, or 'wicca' as it is sometimes called, from the Anglo-Saxon root word *wicce*, which may mean 'wise' but probably means 'bent'! It is usually pronounced 'wicker' as in basket, but really ought to be 'witcha', but no one seems to care.

Modern witches mainly gather in covens to celebrate eight old festivals scattered throughout the year, and hold 'esbats' at the time of the full moon to work magic for healing, luck, divination or sorting out domestic problems. Historically, witches were usually solo workers, serving their village or scattered community as midwives, herbalists, vets, psychic counsellors, layers-out of the dead, and administerers of euthanasia. There is no evidence at all in Britain that covens actually existed, outside the minds of the Christian accusers, from the Stone Age to the present century. Certainly, these secret and powerful people may have met at the old feast days, of which there are at least nine not counting new or full moons, but they left no record of their gatherings in the social history of their now departed world. Here and there are the scattered spells, the buried cat's remains under the hearth, the bottle filled with pins, the simple wooden effigy secreted in the rafters of an old church or house, pointing to the past presence of some magic worker in the area.

Today's covens, with their high priestesses and high priests, are a far cry from the village wisewoman or cunning man, working spells by moonlight, curing cows or warts or broken hearts, with herb and charm. This is not to say that there is no link, but it must be tenuous at best. There was a web of intricate folk magics, green cures, sacred places in remote areas, tingling stones, healing trees and cursing wells; evidence for all of these survives in vast tomes in the Folklore Society's library, in country customs and seasonal fairs, on deserted moors and in many old buildings throughout the land, if you decide to look for their visible ghosts and tangible atmospheres.

Witchcraft or wicca does provide an excellent opportunity for those of likemind to gather to rediscover aspects of pagan religion, making new connections with the ancient but ever-living Gods, sharing the magical rites, dancing and singing in circles, unweaving the tangled skein of arcane lore from its nest of folk tale, song and half-remembered art. Many gain great wisdom from the three-fold path of worship, magic power and craft. But the heart and soul have to be engaged. You cannot be a pagan by mind-power alone, you have to feel the call, experience the desire so strongly that you become free to cast off the conventions of family and upbringing, and name yourself 'witch'. Doing that half-heartedly is a dishonour to the First Parents, the Old Ones of the Wild, the Goddess and her consort of many names.

Unless you really wish to take that road do not make promises or seek initiation to a coven. It is not the path for all and today, many effective and wise witches still work in the traditional way, alone, or with a few chosen companions, at their ancient and simple arts, crafts and natural magics. The Goddess will teach you if you enter her realm in meditation. She will show you the shadows of reality in the moonlight upon still waters, and the sun-bright power of healing and growth. But you must ask, unpriested and alone, in darkness and silence, with a wildly beating heart. She will answer you and take you in, reborn of her family, twice-born Child of Art. Her circle is vast, marked out by the ever-turning stars, lit by the changing moon, warmed by her breath on a summer's night. The nourishing Earth is her altar and her breast, and her song is the voice of the wind.

Whichever path you choose, and there are many more than these briefly outlined above, you must recognise that you will have to spend a long time and a lot of effort mastering the practical arts of meditation and inner journeying which will take you deep into the heart of your chosen tradition, and also studying the literature, the pictures, the artefacts from these cultures in museums. The power inherent in each system is not lightly got, it has to be earned, its symbols thoroughly understood, its Gods and Goddesses welcomed in their own language, attracted by appropriate offerings. Their landscapes need to be delineated clearly in your mind, and the way they communicate with you, answer your questions or offer guidance needs to be understood by working on it gradually, bit by bit, as you might learn a foreign language or a difficult piece of music.

7 · THE CYCLE OF SEASONAL RITES AND FEASTS

She was conscious of a rhythmical pulsation in space, and with one side of
her mind she knew it was Malcolm's pulse-beats she was feeling, and with
the other side she knew it to be the cosmic rhythm; also she knew that these
things were not two things but one thing, and that the pulse of the man's blood
was made one with the primordial force. . . .

Moon Magic
Dion Fortune

Most people enjoy sharing their ritual occasions with others, if this
is at all possible. The problem often arises when a solo practitioner
wishes to celebrate some festival or personal anniversary but his
family either do not know about his magical activities, or they
disapprove. The lone magician may find himself in a quandary,
wishing on the one hand to involve his nearest and dearest in
some mutual festivity, yet wondering if they will laugh at him or
express strong feelings of negativity. It may take a lot of thought
and meditation, but there are certain to be ways round most of the
objections. It is important to stress the ethics of magical ritual, that
rites are performed to heal, to inspire and to grant understanding,

rather than, as the tabloid press would prefer, to curse, to harm and to dominate the wills of other people.

You might well like to celebrate a birthday with a carefully prepared meal at which the table decorations reflect some arcane symbolism. An outdoor picnic with the children can be turned partly to Nature lesson and partly to seasonal celebration, when songs or stories are shared which tell of the Earth Mother and her children, and the magical things which are happening as the seasons turn. The obvious times for parties include Christmas with all its pagan symbolism untouched by the addition of the birth of the Christ child, and Hallowe'en, when ghosts and witches are expected to be abroad, and traditional games like apple bobbing and seeing the future in mirrors are natural parts of the entertainment. Expect to have your leg pulled if you decide to join the youngsters in dressing up as a panto witch or wizard, or if you prepare black jelly with lychees floating in it, to look like eyeballs: How about a Black Feast of caviar on rye bread, black olives, black pudding, dark currant cake, washed down with sweet black Turkish coffee, or dark red Château Neuf du Pape wine, or our native elderberry? It might be a strange mixture, but it would certainly break the ice. Other Hallowe'en colours include purple and orange, and a few plastic bats hung from the ceiling could make the party go with a real swing!

Humour has always been an important facet in the character of the successful magician. It can get him out of tight corners, and if he is very anxious about any kind of working a quiet joke can relieve the tension and allow him to relax fully into his magical self. It is often a useful response to those who attack the beliefs or experiences of occult students to turn their accusations into a joke, by exaggerating something, or comparing the oddity of esoteric subjects to something amusing, like the growing of giant leeks or breeding pink budgies. No one thinks that followers of those uncommon activities are mad or dangerous; why should they imagine that students of the ancient mysteries, mythologies or folk customs are particularly extraordinary either?

If you begin to examine the natural cycle of festivals which was celebrated in Britain and much of Europe, and still continues in some places to this day, you may find that you are able to align yourself with the light and dark times, the feasts and famines, the times of active outward magics and the periods of inward drawing of power and meditation. You can add your own particular regular anniversaries, or those occasional events to which some kind of ritual might be appropriate, like weddings, births or funerals.

SPRING

It is probably easier to begin with the start of the zodiacal year at the first point of Aries at the spring equinox, about 21st March (these solar dates can move a day or two, so check with this year's ephemeris to be exact) when the day is equal to the night. Look at the land around you and see the daffodils and yellow spring flowers, the emerging green spikes hazing some of the early leafing shrubs and misting the bare brown fields with a veil of new growth. It was traditionally the time when seeds were sown, and many of the customs and symbols of Easter were transplanted from older roots to join the Christian festival. The eggs and chicks emerging at this time at Mother Nature's bidding, the magical hares fighting in the fields, which commerce has transmuted into chocolate rabbits, and the obvious return of life to the sleeping Earth are all very ancient symbols. Many of these things can be interwoven into a Spring Ceremony, a celebration of shaking off winter's icy claw and emerging into the solar New Year, refreshed and cleansed. Magically it is a time of growth and expansion, when plans hatched in winter can begin to come into effect and the skills learned from books indoors can be taken out into the wider world.

The next feast is the pagan Beltane, the Good Fire or the Fire of the Sky God, and this should only be celebrated when the Goddess of Earth is dressed in her new white gown of scented hawthorn blossoms. It is the marriage of Heaven and Earth, from which union will come forth the Child of Promise at Yuletide. It is a time of rejoicing, binding the sky power down into the Earth by entwining the patterns of ribbons about the flower-decked May Pole, drawing the healing and warming rays of the Sun into our hearts and spirits, as the days lengthen and grow brighter. Many of the traditional healing herbs are to be seen by now, and the dandelions are gilding the fields and hedgerows, ready for wine. Bluebells are reflecting the sky in the depths of the greenwood and Robin Hood, son of Pan, brother to Jack in the Green, is at large with his beloved Marian.

SUMMER

Time passes until the shortest night, St. John's Eve, when the mid-summer bonfires shower sparks into the sky many a sacred place has visitors, who come to celebrate, share food and wine, sing and dance, and worship older Gods. Many flock to Stonehenge, drawn to this ancient sacred site to watch the Sun rise among the stones, in some unconscious pilgrimage of light. Some bring joy and peace, others discover in the shortened dark a wildness in the blood and feelings they cannot contain. It was a time of battle, when the Sun of summer fought the Dark of winter and was cast down, to dwindle slowly with the waning year. This is reflected in the Mummer's Play, the Tale of Gawaine and the Green Knight, the Goddess's own champion, and many a mystery play.

Lammastide, when the harvest begins and the first loaf is baked from the new-milled corn, is the root of many ancient customs. The last sheaf of corn was cut by lot, and its tall strands were woven into the Kern King, the corn dolly, in the local shape and pattern. This special symbol would be set in a place of honour inside the house until next year's sowing, when its magical seeds would ensure plenty in the cycle then begun. The Harvest Home, culmination of the farmer's year with its traditional songs, is being revived, partly as a tourist entertainment, in some places it is a recollection of the times gone by, and reconnects us to our natural cycle of light and dark, summer and winter, sleep and wakefulness.

Autumn

The next main time of feasting is Michaelmas, around the time of the autumnal equinox when night and day fall into balance, and when the fatted goose is brought from the empty harvest field to deck the table in the dining hall. St. Michael is a Sun God in borrowed garb, and his hilltop churches mark the line of setting sun or rising light across the land. He was once called Gwyn ap Nudd, Light born of Night, and battled with another saint for the entrance of his hidden domain, below Glastonbury's magic Tor.

This is a time of personal harvesting, gathering in those achievements and failures, those successes and let-downs, to be examined and weighed at this time of balanced light. From those things which are found to be good and worthwhile will come the seeds of next year's enterprise, the hopes and desires for another cycle of growth and work.

Next comes Hallowe'en, a time of divination and preparation for the winter's rest and inward-looking arts. This was the Celtic New Year, for they calculated their time by nights, and this was the eve of the year itself. We have the expression 'a fortnight', meaning fourteen nights, with us still.

This was a period of reckoning, of assessing the value of the harvest, of sorting out the breeding stock of cattle and sheep, and culling some to be salted down for winter food. It was a time of gathering the family together, to take counsel, to greet the new children, to mourn and say farewell to the departed souls, yet at this time when the veil between now and hereafter is thin, to speak with them also, to hear what the ancestors might offer in terms of instruction or advice.

Many of the games played at Hallowe'en parties have very ancient roots. The apple was the Celtic tree of immortality. Its silvery branch was the sure passport for those who wished to visit fairyland, and return again, its fruits concealed a mystery, and it was known as the Tree of Knowledge. Those who could seize the swinging apple on its string or, without completely drowning, fetch an apple in their teeth from the water butt would have luck, success and plenty in the coming months. The apple peel, cut in one long strand and cast over the left shoulder, would predict the initial of a new love or partner. The chestnuts set upon the hearth, inscribed with marks, would indicate true loves and false by bursting with a crack.

WINTER

Just as November 5th still fills the sky with lights and bonfires flare on every hill, so did our ancestors welcome in the winter tide. With exploding conkers in fires and other nuts set to roast or burst, they too would greet the returning traveller, who might just be the Goddess in disguise. The 17th century celebration of the failure of the Gunpowder Plot was but a new style of an older feast, at which effigies were offered to the fire, including the wicker man, filled with the remnants of failures and old wrongs. The Romans accused the Druids of burning people in baskets, but did not recognise that the empty wicker shape was the symbol of those outgrown things, those worthless bits of mental and physical rubbish that could be cleared away before the dark of winter. The meat was not some pagan victim, burned alive, but the carcass of a slaughtered beast, butchered for the table lest it starve in the empty fields and bitter snowbound hills. It was the last festival of plenty, before the time of Yule.

Yule, the Saxon name derived from 'wheel', sees another turn of the season's spiral path. Now was the birth of the Star Child, in a lowly place, a stall among the beasts, as were born many gods, Mithras, Horus and the rest, light-bringers, Sons of the Sun, and hope for all the world.

Yet this was also a time of anxiety and concern, for people might have thought, 'What happens if the Sun does not return? What will we do if the days shorten until there is no light left?'. And from the longest night for about four or five nights there was great effort, through magic, through lighting fires, and making prayers and offerings of green leaves, until gradually the night began to shorten. Then was held the Great Feast of the Return of Light, originally the birthday of Mithras, a Persian Sun God, now Jesus, each born in a lowly cave. It is for this reason that services are held at midnight and not dawn on Christmas Day, in recollection of those worried pagans, whose time was marked from night to night, awaiting the strengthening of the Sun.

It was always a time of gathering, feasting and giving small gifts. Many of the decorations and characters of the Yule season have very ancient roots in Celtic or Norse tradition. The holly was sacred to the God of the Green and the Ivy, white-flowered, was dedicated to the Goddess, whose priestesses chewed just enough of its poisonous leaves to become her inspired oracles. The magical mistletoe, when found growing on an oak tree, was a great sign of healing and revelation to the Druids. To this day few churches, save York Minster, will allow it in their Christmas garlands. It is still used as a potent herbal drug.

For twelve days the Yule log smouldered on the hearth, the mighty root of an oak tree, or the lighter ashen faggot burned where oaks do not grow. For twelve days the Child of Promise grew a year a day until, as was thought right in earlier ages, he began to take on those adult marks, his proper name, his bow and spear and sword, and the secret knowledge of his people, growing to become the young God who would lead them through the next year's cycle of life. His departure was recalled in the Feast of Epiphany, 6th January by modern calendars, when the three Magi, the astrologer priests, having followed the star, found the young Christ Child still in the lowly stable, and offered the sacred gifts of gold, frankincense and myrrh. Gold for sovereignty on earth, frankincense to honour the priestly role, and myrrh whose white and bitter smoke conjures spirits and foretells the sacrifice to come.

This is an important date in the pagan year, but it is largely overlooked by modern witches. To the magician it should be a day of commitment, of looking back and then casting out those things which are no longer needed, and of learning from the Goddess the next step of inner work. Imagine, in a pathworking perhaps, that the three wise men are passing your way and can advise you, teach you or grant you knowledge. Or that you stand at the Goddess's knee, a magical child, and she is teaching you the secrets of your heritage, giving you the keys to the wisdom of the ancestors.

The last of the sequence of traditional festivals is that of Candlemas, St. Bridget or Imbolc, at the beginning of February, when the first flowers were seen, usually snowdrops in Britain. This was the time when the Goddess would grant favours, and the women of the household would deck out a place beside the hearth, that home altar in all old houses, with bright scarves and early flowers and greenery. They would treat the invisible Goddess as a guest, baking a special cake and preparing wine or possibly ewe's milk, as the Celtic name of the festival is Oimelc, ewe's milk. (Sheep milk was drunk and made into cheeses and was just as valuable as the fleece or meat.) After the women had met alone, the men would also come and ask for help with practical skills through the year.

Most of this cycle of ancient festivals has now been fossilised by being firmly attached to calendar dates. None of these feasts ought to be fixed except by the Sun entering a sign of the zodiac, particularly at the solstices and equinoxes. That moment needs to be discovered from the current ephemeris, and the other sequence of feasts decided from the works of Mother Nature herself. When the first snowdrop is seen in your garden, then you can celebrate; when the may blossom whitens the hedge, welcome the date of the Goddess's marriage feast. Then when the first corn is reaped and its grain ground for flour and the first loaf baked you can celebrate Lammas. Hallowe'en is the night after the first frost which whitens the grass and clearly indicates summer is ended, hence its Celtic name, Samhain (pronounced *sow-in*).

You will be able to add in more dates throughout the year to make an individual cycle of celebration, remembrances, anniversaries, births, marriages and deaths. You can focus your magical attention on every new and full moon, using the Goddess in her triple aspects to awaken psychic powers and open those inner doors to inspiration and imagination. You may work only withthe esoteric tides of Cleansing after Yule, Growing to midsummer, Reaping to the autumnal equinox, and Repose into the winter. Although ordinary people are not aware of the great universal forces sweeping through their lives, the tides flow right through the pattern of everyday events. Certain times of the year, particularly January and August, seem to be when you hear of deaths; at other times there are more births and lucky events. When you step

93

upon the magical road, willingly or not, those tides will begin to affect your own pattern too.

DAY AND NIGHT

The other shorter and far more obvious cycle, which again is important to all serious magical folk, is that of day and night. Those who find their way into one of the schools or lodges of high magic will come under a strict and probably lifelong discipline of daily salutations or recognitions. This is a perpetual cycle of moments of silent meditation to be performed on waking, or at dawn to be correct; at solar noon, which may be 1.00 pm (according to British Summer Time) or local time variations; and either at sunset or on going to bed. This sets a natural pattern of awareness, marking your relationship with the Light, symbolised by the rising, noon-tide and setting Sun. If you are about, you can add a midnight salutation to the Goddess, whose starry mantle wraps the world before sleep and whose elusive rays inspire dreams and visions.

The dawn prayer may be for strength through the day or any kind of practical help. At noon it is usually a matter of brief acknowledgement of the hour, a blink of attuned consciousness as you sit down to lunch, a moment of mental alignment to the work and all those who walk the inner paths. At dusk or on retiring there should be a longer exercise of meditation, reviewing your daily tasks, mentally completing those things undone, preparing your mind for sleep. Often the discipline expects a period of ongoing and symbolic meditation at least once a day, on some theme or image concerned with the work or training a student is undergoing.

Those who work alone should be willing to practise self-discipline along similar lines, for the regular structure of meditation and attunement does really help these skills to develop and come under conscious control. Such focused moments of mental effort also make the awareness of time very acute; you find you do not need your digital watch to chime the noon hour, but know it, and you come to recognise the moment of the full or new moon also, if you work with those changing tides. Allow this perception to grow so that you intuitively recognise the right moment to begin a ritual, and the time to complete it. It may sound far-fetched, but we do all have amazingly accurate inner awareness of the passing of time. Experiments with hypnotised subjects have often demonstrated this, when they are given a post-hypnotic command to act so many moments, hours, even days later, yet they fulfil this request to the exact minute. A magician brings this ability into conscious control, so that he can awaken at any time, to beat the alarm clock or to greet the dawn of a special day, or perform some rare, nocturnal rite.

PRIEST OF THE RITES

One of the functions of the magician is that of the priest. This is a fairly rare calling, but many pagans who are initiated into witchcraft are called 'witch and priest/priestess' by the words of the ritual. It is one of the aspects of working with the inner realms, with the powers of the Gods and Goddesses as facets of the Creator, that is seldom discussed, yet it is a genuine part of our arcane heritage. Being a priest or shaman or Guide to the Inner Ways is a job that may become far more important in the New Age, when a fresh religious and spiritual impulse will affect many people. Carl Jung was convinced that one of the primal urges in mankind was that of worship and religious obligation. We may have satisfied many of our mundane wants, for home and partner and settled existence, but the spirit is hungry and the technological twentieth century does not satisfy the soul.

It is unlikely that a new messiah will arrive, but rather that each awoken individual will come to recognise the Light within, the sacred power of life and love and healing that can be tapped and shared. When Jesus performed his acts of healing he told his followers, 'These things, and greater than these shall you do . . .'. We have managed to overlook this teaching, but an awareness that the power of the Creator can be found within us may well be a gift offered to the future when the New Age dawns. We all have immense talents which we do not use; we have skills and crafts and spiritual powers which are largely untested. Those who walk the paths of magic are few, those who strive for spiritual awareness are not always properly assisted towards their individual potential. As with any other commodity which can be marketed and from which a profit can be reaped, there will be 'gurus' or 'schools' or even material objects like videos or books which 'guarantee' salvation or instant enlightenment. Sadly, there are those who are desperate for guidance, who will buy these useless things. Any kind of spiritual awakening has to come from within and, like a seed growing secretly in the dark earth, needs to be tended with gentleness and care.

The magical world has not escaped exploitation, for on all levels there are unscrupulous people whose prime aim in life is the fast buck, no matter who is harmed by this. At one level there are the purveyors of 'Miracle Cures' or 'Amazing Magical Talismans' at a price. At another there are offered extremely expensive courses of instruction which demean the students, frighten them and cause them to become unsettled. Those who offer these things are aware of the consequences of their actions but they are willing to prey on the weaknesses of people, especially at times of great change or bereavement. A new magical current is needed to counteract that dark flood which misrepresents our sacred arts and artefacts.

Those who take up magic seriously take upon their shoulders an ancient and heavy burden of responsibility. Every action in magic, as in physics, has an equal and opposite reaction. If you wish for something and get it, that thing has to be taken from someone else. In ethical work, that thing must be discarded by its previous owner, freely. It may not be stolen nor coerced, although it may be bought for a true price, to be paid in cash or kind, in the marketplace. As every act has a purpose, it must also have a price of responsibility. If you heal, then be aware what sort of life the healed person may be going back to. Has he learned what the illness can teach in terms of patience, care or the value of well-being? If you bring people together or bind them through rites of handfasting, how clearly can you see their linked futures? For a year? For a lifetime or forever? Some pagan priests commit people to each other for eternity – a foolish and short-sighted promise.

Priests for the New Age will need to take up a very ancient role, not merely as one who stands between the people and their Gods, passing messages one way and prayers the other, but as one who learns the arts of true and spiritual healing,of wise counsel and practical forgiveness, within the laws of karma, where that which was wronged must be righted by the same hand, in this life or another. The priestess must show that all forgiveness begins in the heart, and that only love and care for self can offer absolution. The new priesthood will have to learn to open the doors of awareness gently in the flock who come for such spiritual comfort. Through guidance on inner journeys to the heart of the myth or the soul of the hearer, the wise ones will lead each individual to the place of personal blessing, spiritual cleansing and peace. They will teach of the life everlasting, through the pattern of incarnations, and show those who are ready for the journey the other side of death, both from their past experiences and perhaps for future transitions into the life beyond. It is no easy task, nor is it light, for those who have never walked upon the inner ways may regard such theories as dangerous, un-Christian or unacceptable. There can be no coercion, nor should anyone be made to give up long-held beliefs on religious or spiritual matters.

There may come a time when there is room for sacred sanctuaries where marriages may be solemnised, children named and blessed, and the departed bidden farewell, until their next life. At present many covens do perform such rituals within their own pagan tradition, ceremonies of handfasting, of 'paganing' young children, of initiating consenting adults into their art, and of bidding farewell at the crematorium to those who have died. Many of the recent books of rituals for modern witches include the texts for these ceremonies, but they do seem to fit best within the coven's own circle, when only witches are involved. However, if you decide that the priesthood appeals to your spirit, you can set about designing rituals for these and other purposes.

Religion has to be a personal thing. You will have to work hard on your individual beliefs, experiences and philosophy before you can discuss them, let alone share them, with others. In the occult world where an acceptance of a great Creator is a vital aspect of the reality of magic, the form in which that Creator is envisaged, how it/he/she is approached, can vary a great deal. It is quite acceptable to acknowledge many Gods and Goddesses, of a traditional or personal pantheon, and a cycle of festivals can be celebrated, but such celebrations have to be sincere and heartfelt, not a matter of going through the actions to keep in step with some religious sect, orthodox or pagan. You will have to spend much time in individual communion with your deities, in prayer, meditation, in fast and vigil, if that fits into your scheme of things, and not merely pay lip service to someone else's creed. Occult work is based on sound knowledge, practical experience and personal revelation, not regurgitated beliefs forced on you by some external source.

The other aspect of the esoteric philosophies which needs a lot of thought before you launch yourself into the company of doubting and challenging friends concerns the whole concept of invisible realities, wherein the seeds of practical occult work are sown. You will be asked, time and time again, 'What do you believe?', 'How can you accept that magic spells can work in the twentieth century?', 'What do you mean by gods and goddesses, God is dead, or never lived . . .' Each of these will need to be met with a suitable and carefully thought out response.

We do not need proof of the power of gravity, we do not need proof of the evolution of species, we do not need proof of the ever-changing pattern of the seasons, but we may need to understand, at least to our own satisfaction, the concept of a Creator who still has a care for the physical universe. We need to be able to see that the whole cosmos is interconnected. We are made of the stuff of stars, we are part of Earth, and by our very physical form are united with all other parts of Earth, the trees, the animals, the rocks and minerals, and all the life forms too small or too ephemeral to be noticed. It is with those shared links that our magic can work; the changes or evolutions which we wish to happen occur as real, physical processes because we too are evolving.

The priestly function may be one of the more public aspects of New Age occult work, and is not the path many may wish to tread. The other obvious direction lies within the safe and comfortable fellowship of an occult society, school or lodge, or a witches' coven. Here is always the best opportunity for training, for sharing rituals and celebrations and gaining the confidence to work your own magic. By receiving individual guidance from those who have walked your chosen path before you, and by being in the company of others with whom you may compete for position and against whom you can judge yourself, your progress might seem swift and easy. This is not the case, however, for the path you choose will have to be walked alone, the speed at which you make progess will be individual to you, the time by which you are ready to recognise and handle power cannot be measured in earthly days or months, but on a scale of inner hours.

Ultimately you will have to be your own companion, and befriend those inner powers, the ancient deities, those hidden aspects of self which can teach, heal and guide you through the changing pattern of ritual observances, celebrations, rites of remembrance, communion with the Gods, and dedication and empowerment of talismans. The feasts you choose to acknowledge, the prayers you might make, requests or thanksgiving you may offer up, eventually have to be those you need.

EXERCISE TEN – THE SACRED CYCLE

Draw on a large sheet of paper the largest circle you can fit in, using a dinner plate or cake tin, etc. Divide it into twelve segments to represent the months. Enter in each month the things which you might wish to celebrate, the pagan feasts, birthdays, anniversaries, dates of death, of initiations or degrees (which in a way give you a new 'birthday' at each level) and any other data which seems relevant. From next year's ephemeris or a good diary, write in the dates of new and full moons, the equinoxes in March and September, the solstices in December and June, and any other astral information, like eclipses or times of planetary conjunction, and comets which you might find in books on astronomy.

Begin to fill in each segment of the circle with flowers or plants, with Gods or Goddesses, heroes or mythological figures, which to you represent the month. Mark the edges of the circle with different colours to represent the element which rules each sign of the zodiac, if you are interested in astrology.

When you have entered all you know now, write a list of themes for monthly meditation, or the kinds of rituals you might work then. You may find that discovering the planet which rules each sign of the zodiac will help you find uses for each month's inherent power. Plan ahead for any seasonal rites, collecting natural flowers or leaves to deck your altar, or a vase in your home, or bring in symbolic objects to help focus your magic. You will also need to begin to make out your Book of Illumination, which should be a large loose-leaf file. In this can be preserved the words, actions, diagrams or pressed flowers used at any ritual you work, and notes of visions seen, results observed, and steps of inner growth discovered. This book and the accompanying circular plan should be kept to hand throughout your yearly work, so that you do not forget what season you are in or what symbols might be needed, and so that you can often refer back to the results of last year's efforts, or at least work done six months ago.

8 · THE RITE APPROACH

Advanced rituals should not, therefore, use vast arrays of physical objects, nor should they rely upon technology for matters that belong within the imagination. In other words, we should not need objects to stimulate our inner energies through association. Advanced magical arts reverse this process, and the inner energies sanctify or endow the chosen objects with required properties. This is a very ancient magical concept indeed, and needs to be kept firmly in mind for practical work.

Advanced Magical Arts
R.J. Stewart

All magical ritual is a matter of pulling together a variety of threads of knowledge and practical arts to weave the pattern of the creation of change, and that change causes the magic to come to fulfilment. That is why the old notion of 'spell weaving', 'weaving enchantments' and 'binding runes' still holds true. One level of this, invisible to our everyday eyes, is the creation of the setting within our mind's eye, and the ability to hold the picture right through the working. Even if you have an actual temple, fully set out with an altar, pillars, banners and all the officers in full regalia, you have to build over this the inner temple. The following exercise will provide you with an appropriate setting for most Western rituals, so long as you fully focus your attention on 'seeing' it, bit by bit. Later on you will learn to alter some aspects to suit your own particular work.

EXERCISE ELEVEN – APPROACHING THE TEMPLE

This is an inner journey narrative. It isn't something to read, but to be worked. Each aspect has a powerful inner meaning so you should either ask one of your companions to read the text, or read it yourself onto a cassette tape, always pausing for the slow count of four at every full stop. You may find you need to pause longer to begin with, until your concentration is sufficient to be able to see, hear, smell, touch and taste every relevant part of the setting. This does matter. Unless you are able to sense these inner realms you will have no control over your magic or your dreams.

Learn, bit by bit, first to relax with your eyes closed, and then to fully awaken that interior sight which will help you gradually perceive what is described, and it is a real landscape and building. If you can't manage it all at once, the first few times you should aim to 'see' the journey, then the arrival at the outside of the building. Then add the entry and finally the entire scene, recalling every detail and returning to your normal waking state gently, by reversing as much of the journey as you have managed. If you are in the fortunate position of having several companions to share your training, then take it in turns to read the narrative, or each learn by heart a certain aspect of it, so that you can share out the descriptive text. At the same time, allowing your companions to add in details which they become aware of will enhance the experience for all of you. A tape can be used for a group, of course.

Preparation
Find a place where you will not be disturbed for at least half an hour, shut off the phone, light a candle and incense if you like it. Set out a pen and paper to record any ideas or images that come to you afterwards, and a drink and snack to help you return to Earth at the end. Sit upright in a supportive chair, close your eyes, relax, and breathe slowly and deeply for at least ten breaths. Become poised and attentive, whilst allowing everyday distractions to fade from your awareness. Be absolutely still and remain so, no matter why you might want to move. Relax some more. It is important that you become thoroughly used to the adventure, and remain relaxed but very aware. Now start the tape, or if you are reading the text, begin very slowly (Don't forget to count slowly to four at each full stop).

The Journey

We are going on an inner journey to the Temple of the Western Tradition. You find yourself, to begin with, on a grassy hillside, on a narrow, twisting path. There are many wild flowers in the tall grass on each side of the path, and you can hear the wind rustling through them. You may also smell them, and the distant drift of new mown hay. It is a warm sunny afternoon and you are looking forward to visiting the Temple where your magic can become a reality.

The path winds on between the rolling, grassy hills until you begin to see, in the distance, a cluster of low stone buildings. They are surrounded by trees and a garden bright with flowers, divided from the wild flowery meadows by a neatly trimmed hedge. The path flattens out before the gate of the enclosure and a figure dressed in a light grey cloak comes to meet you. You cannot see his or her face which is concealed by a deep hood. The voice, when it welcomes you, is warm and low. You are told to follow the guide to the places you most want to visit. First you are led through the gardens, some bright with summer flowers, others green and aromatic with herbs. Fruit trees abound, standing alone, or spread along walls of pale golden stone which surround the buildings. All are in full summer leaf, and new buds and fruits are visible on every green leafy branch.

Always your guide walks beside you, pointing out the various sorts of plants, telling you their uses in food, or medicine, or in opening the inner eye of true vision, burning sweetly in incenses, or scenting the air.

Ahead of you, you begin to see a building of pale, honey-gold stone, with an arched doorway raised above a low flight of steps. Your guide points at the closed door, made from great oak planks, bound with bronze hinges and fittings. Here you must go on alone. You climb the wide, shallow steps, and raise a knocker of bronze, made in the shape of a Celtic Cross, and let it fall. The echoes fade inside the building. Slowly, guided by unseen hands, the door swings open. Inside it is very dark. There is a passage leading into the building, and where light falls from behind you, you see that the floor is alternate squares of black and white stone slabs. You enter, and feel the air is cooler than outside. It is very dim, and as your eyes grow accustomed to the shade, you smell sweet incense, old stone and sacredness.

Alone you walk slowly into the passage. Ahead you begin to

make out a small light. On either side you pass doors. Most of them are closed but one opens onto a room in which you see many shelves of books, reaching to the low ceiling. The scent of ancient paper, cobwebs and leather bindings seeps into your nostrils. You carry on towards the tiny spark of light, but you are stopped in your tracks by a filmy curtain of dark blue material, through which the point of light glimmers. You know you must brush aside this flimsy barrier, but you need a moment to gather your courage. Silently you ask permission to be allowed into the Holy Place. You lift the edge of the curtain and walk through.

Before you a large, square stone room opens out. It is dimly lit and there seem to be no windows. Looking down you see that the floor is now all black, but that tiny points of silver mark the stations of the stars in the familiar constellations, ringing a central altar.

There are no other visitors. It is very quiet, yet musical sounds seem to fill the air as if a choir were singing wordlessly in some other part of the building. Incense smoulders nearby, and its thick and scented clouds further dim the dark room. You look about you and see that this magical Temple is square, with plain light-coloured stone walls. The ceiling is curved into a natural dome, and is black or dark blue. The stars there reflect those in the floor, and all sparkle.

The door by which you entered is not central to the wall, but set off slightly to the side, and you see next to it a low table, covered with a deep green cloth. On the centre of the table is set a large and rugged rock of some white mineral.

You turn to your left and, following a faint trail of stars on the floor, proceed a quarter circle. Here you find another table, covered with a golden cloth. Upon it is a polished bronze incense burner, in the deep heart of which charcoal glows and spicy incense smoke rises. You notice too a rod of wood, entwined with the shapes of snakes, one pale, one dark, looking so real you dare not touch them. In the smoky light their eyes glitter brightly.

Now you continue your slow journey another quarter circle, until you encounter another table, covered with a scarlet cloth. On it burns an elaborate bronze oil lamp whose flame rises still and golden in the quiet temple. In the flames gold light, the silver reflections from a long dagger blade shine against the red cloth. The hilt is shaped like two dragons, facing outwards, with their tails making the handle. The grip is red leather, worn smooth, and the end of the hilt is formed of a ball of crystal enclosed in a silver net. For a few moments you stand spellbound, and your breathing makes the flame flutter and the details of the sword shift and shine.

Again you go on, following the starry path beneath your feet, to the next quarter, and there is a table covered with a sea-blue cloth. Upon it stands a great bowl of crystal filled with clear water. In it dance points of flame from the lamps. Beside it stands a beautiful chalice of silver, filled with dark red wine. You pick out the Celtic interlace patterns engraved on its surface, and the inlays of gold and precious stones. You feel the sacredness of this cup, and something wells up within you, filling your heart with emotion, and your eyes with tears.

Getting a grip on your feelings you walk another quarter circle, back to the place of the green robed table. Now you notice, beside the strange quartz rock, there is a simple wooden platter, carved with leaves and flowers. Upon it lies a small chunk of rough bread, and a pinch of grainy white salt. You feel strong and well balanced and calm.

Now you look to the centre of the Temple, seeing clearly with your dark-adapted eyes the central altar. It is draped with a cloth of indigo velvet and its surface is almost bare. Above it, on chains of bronze, hangs a clear glass vessel of oil with its floating wick offering the first gleam of light which drew you to this holy sanctuary. As you draw near, the sounds of distant chanting increase and a great upwelling of feeling grows inside you.

You stand before the altar in this sacred and ancient place, and looking down, see another mystery. On the top of the indigo cloth there is a small square of violet, and in the centre of that is a circle of shining darkness. It might be a black mirror, it might be a secret reflection of a clear moonless night sky, magically brought down into the heart of the Temple. For a while you stand transfixed. Perhaps you almost feel you are falling into the dark, becoming a star among stars in the firmament. Pause for a few moments.

Suddenly your hand brushes against the velvet altar cloth and your reverie is broken. It may have lasted a mere moment, or an hour. You have no way of telling. What you have seen in the dark glass, or experienced in the night sky, will stay in your memory, to be reflected upon later. Now it is time to return and as you make up your mind, a soft rustle of the curtain at the doorway signals that your guide is waiting for you. In reverence and slight

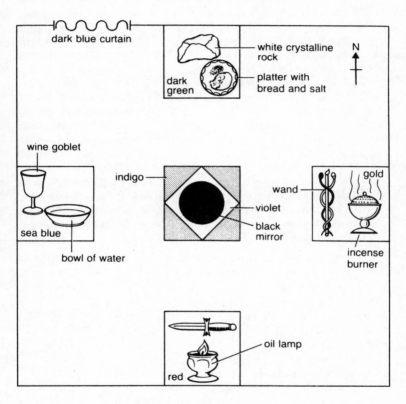

The Temple

awe you walk to the doorway, and the cloaked guide lifts the curtain and lets it fall behind you.

You stand in the dark corridor for a while, getting your bearings, and then the guide escorts you to the great wooden door. He or she pulls it open, letting in the bright light of afternoon, and you are dazzled. As you go out into the light you are stopped at the top of the steps by your guide's hand on your shoulder. You are being offered something; it is a key, which will open the mighty bronze-bound door, and permit you to return to this Temple of the Western Mysteries. You take the key and it seems to melt into your hand. You look up to say thanks, but now you are alone.

Before you the path stretches smooth and winding, among the scented herbs and flowering plants, outward to the green hills. As you walk away from the honey-gold buildings the pictures of what you have seen, the experiences of what you have felt, the inner revelations of what you have briefly been a part of deepen in your awareness.

Gradually you return to your own body, breathing deeply and calmly. Allow yourself a time of gentle awakening, returning bit by bit to full and conventional consciousness. You have been on a long journey, and will need time to assimilate the experience, write your notes, become attuned to the everyday world again. And this is only the beginning.

Although this exercise may seem simple and straightforward if you are merely reading the text, when it is worked as a magical ritual it will show the power of symbolism. Each part of it needs many sessions of thought and meditation. If you are not in a position to set up a real room as a temple, this imagery will work in its stead. If there is a sacred space within your home, then this Inner Temple may be transposed over it, to bring power and balance and the ancient forces of the elements into and around your working.

The exercise should be attempted only once in a day, and not for more than three days in a row, until you are really able to enter into it and feel comfortable there. It is a real place, founded long ago as the centre of Western magic, ritual and wisdom. Each time you return there you may be able to explore the buildings, for apart from the Temple and library which you have glimpsed in this journey, there are classrooms and laboratories, gardens and halls for magical ritual and for quiet meditation.

SETTING UP YOUR OWN TEMPLE

Study the text and the setting of the Inner Temple. Every facet is part of an ancient and potent Mystery, from the black and white pavement to the altar cloths, and the symbols of the Quarters. From the description above you can learn how to set out your own working space, if there is enough room. If you don't have small tables at each Quarter (cheap bedside cabinets are ideal, for incenses and books, altar cloths and regalia may be kept in them), a candlestick, a coloured mat and the relevant symbol or instrument may be placed on the floor.

It does help to have an actual central altar, on which various things need to be placed. This should ideally be a double cube in shape, as high as your solar plexus, but any round or square table, etc., can be used. Even things as strange as large audio speakers, back to back, have been used, as well as flower stands or chests of drawers. What is needed is a flat, firm surface at least two feet square. If you intend to burn incense or lighted candles it is worth ensuring that tiles or stone slabs are provided for these. Another answer is to get a piece of plate glass and put that on top of the altar cloth, so that spilled oil, water or wine, or upset flames will do no harm.

When you open your own circle, you may wish to call upon the Guardians of the Quarters from a particular system. These may be the Qabalistic Angels, the Elemental Kings, the Four Winds (as used by the Alexandrian witches) or any other set of Gods and Goddesses or symbolic characters who will protect and empower your working. If you are using names of deities, please find out exactly what they are concerned with, what their names mean, and don't assume because you have read it in a book that these will either be safe or will respond to you at all! Meditate, and if you still aren't certain then don't use them. Simply ask that the Goddess of Earth or Water, and the God of Fire or Air, attend you and help. Even these basic concepts may be varied in certain traditions!

It is best to get to know the pattern of ritual and to gradually collect prayers, invocations, poems and music to suit each Quarter, according to your chosen tradition or personal choice. If possible, write the words yourself, even if they are not especially poetic or lengthy. Learn to speak aloud, even if you are alone, and pitch your voice lower to add resonance until you master the art of chanting or intoning sacred words.

107

An invocation calls down from the height both those elevated powers to whom you will be addressing your requests and the highest aspect of your inner self, to work in harmony to facilitate your magic. Evocations tend to do the opposite, calling up lower energies which are difficult to control and causing your own protective barriers (a part of your higher self) to be set aside, so that you are very vulnerable

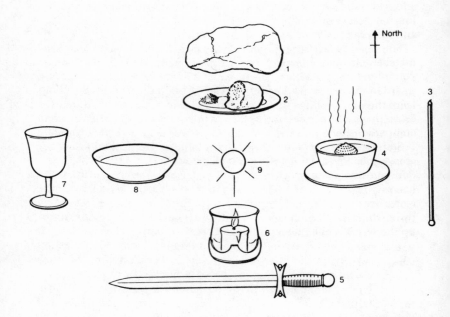

The Altar
1. Rock 2. Platter with bread and salt 3. Wand 4. Incense burner
5. Sword or Dagger 6. Nightlight or Lamp 7. Chalice or Goblet
8. Bowl of water 9. Central light (may be suspended overhead)

to unpleasant and unsettling energies, stirred up like the muddy waters at the bottom of a pond. Until you have had at least three years' solid magical training and work, don't play with this ancient, and recently rather neglected, aspect of magical work. You can't rely on adepts on white chargers coming to your rescue as they may do in films or novels!

A SIMPLE CEREMONY

Just to give you some idea of the sort of thing you will need to practise and feel happy with, here is a simple ceremony, based on the Inner Journey described in Exercise Eleven, with an added invocation poem and instructions as to what to do.

You need to start by getting all your equipment together, candles, matches, incense, bread, wine, platters, dagger/sword and wand, if you intend to use these, and copying out the words in big letters onto a card to carry round with you. If you are really dedicated you should learn the words – these aren't 'gospel', it is better to make up your own and if they rhyme they are easier to remember. Set up your altar, chair, companions, etc. Relax!

Start the journey, speaking slowly and imagining each phase, the grassy meadows, the smooth path, the distant building. Enter the door and the passage, and continue until the point where the guide leaves you to enter the sacred place alone. Stand up and go to the North-western position. Turn to your left and acknowledge the North by bowing slightly, then go on clockwise to the East. If possible, raise up the wand whilst you speak, facing outwards, to the East. Say:

> Wand of the Air, in the day's first hour,
> Bringer of Light from the East, grant me(us)
> power!

Put down the wand at the Eastern edge of the circle, on a table if there is one, and light the first candle at the Quarter. If you have an incense burner or some joss sticks in a proper holder, light these also. Take your time. Obviously, if you have companions they should share the work and the words. You may carry the instrument round the circle if you like.

Then go to the South, face out, raise up the sword or dagger or flame symbol (lamp, etc.) and say:

> *Illumine my (our) life (lives), Southern Blade of Flame,*
> *At noon may danger vanish at your name.*

Then light that candle, and if there is a special lamp, light that too and carry it to the central altar (or light the altar lamp now).

Then go to the West, face out and say, as you raise the cup of water:

> *Flowing waters of the Western Sea,*
> *Let your eventide chalice grant me (us) purity!*

You can carry this cup around the circle flicking water or sprinkling it with a sprig of rosemary. Then light the Western candle.

Then go to the North, pick up the platter or pentacle or other symbol and say:

> *Earthy pentacle of the rocky North,*
> *From night's great darkness send the stars forth.*

Carry the symbol around the circle, replace it in the North and light that candle. Then go to the East, or perhaps walk right round the circle again (or if you haven't been able to do this with each element, do it once now). ending up at the East. Say:

> *Mighty forces circle round, Bless this place as sacred ground,*
> *And as my (our) magic work I (we) start, Enlighten, bless, empower my (our) art!*
> *That I (we) may gain true harmony, As I (we) will it,*
> *SO MAY IT BE!*

Then sit down for a few moments, just making sure that the candles and incense are burning well and safely (relight them now if they aren't). Then meditate for a few moments, seeing each Quarter as it is described in the Journey narrative, especially if you don't have swords, cups, wands and pentacles and are having to make do without these, or with stand-in objects, for example a plate for a pentacle, an ordinary stick for a wand and a carving knife as a sword. These 'stand-ins' will do just as well if you give them the power of the real object.

State the purpose of your ritual and then give it a few moments' silent thought in case you remember anything you had overlooked.

Then continue the working, celebrate the communion. You will need to make up a short invocation to bless the bread/biscuits and salt, if you use these traditional items, and the cup of wine or fruit juice as well. Usually the bread is dedicated to the God or solar power and the wine to the Goddess or power of the Moon, although the tradition in which you are working may have alternative prayers already.

When you have completed all the work, and then waited another few minutes in silence in case there is some kind of revelation or realisation which you can comprehend, you may begin the closing ritual. First you will need a number of short prayers for world peace, healing, justice or any of the eternal virtues which you believe the Earth lacks. You can remember a particular person for healing, or an animal, or some natural disaster, but it is important to use up any residue of power you have raised by these requests for objectives beyond your personal needs. This is how you pay for your magic, by helping others within a wider sphere. If the Earth is sick or being mutilated, because you are made of the same stuff those torments are your problem and do need to be remembered during ritual working!

When you are completely ready to close the ritual and your companions have nothing else to do or say, you can begin by standing up and sensing what energies are still flowing around you. When you can feel this, say:

> *Now this hour's work is done,*
> *By Earth and Star, and Moon and Sun,*
> *Now is the moment for repose,*
> *So gently let this circle close.*

Walk to the North, raise the symbol, and if you wish carry it anti-clockwise round the circle, back to the North, then say:

> *Power of the North, let darkness be,*
> *Grant me (us) the feeling of stability.*

Snuff out the Northern candle there with your fingers or a snuffer.

Walk round to the West and pick up the cup of water. Again this may be carried or even sprinkled in the anti-clockwise direction, then say:

> *Power of the West, of the flowing oceans,*
> *Grant me (us) control of my swift emotions.*

111

Snuff out the Western candle.

Then go round to the South, pick up the lamp or sword, carry it round anti-clockwise, back to the South, and say:

> Power of the South, the flame of Light,
> Grant inner strength by day and night.

Snuff out the candle and the lamp, if you use one.

Go to the East, raise the wand and circle anti-clockwise, and then say:

> Power of the East, with the wind's soft breath,
> Lead me (us) to Light through life and death.

Snuff out the last candle, and turn to face the centre, pausing so that you can feel the flow of power gently sinking down and fading away, and your own sense of the world returning to normal. Then say finally:

> From beneath me (us) may peace arise,
> And flow to all beings beneath the skies.
> So may this be!

That concludes the ritual, but you will need to ensure that the altar lamp is safe, if it is allowed to burn out, and the incense is dead. Empty crumbs of bread, the last drops of wine and the incense ashes out onto a garden if possible, to earth the ritual. The candles from the Quarters may be used each time until they are burned down, but you will need to ensure a supply of charcoal blocks and various incenses, night lights for the altar lamp and perhaps that of the South, as well as matches or a reliable lighter.

The most important thing with any ritual is do it slowly. Speak firmly, quietly and slowly, meaning and understanding every single word. If you borrow other people's rites, do make absolutely certain you know what they mean and what they are intended for. Purpose is all in magic!

EXERCISE TWELVE – CONSECRATING THE INSTRUMENTS OF MAGIC

Collect everything you need and if possible, write a check list in your Book of Illumination. Put on your magical robe (unless that is the item to be consecrated at this ritual). Light the altar lamp and declare it cleansed and dedicated to showing the Light of Truth, Love, Wisdom and Power.

Move to the face of the altar which you have designated as East, light a disc of incense charcoal, allowing it to get properly hot, and set it into a chafing dish or thurible. Add the grains of incense of your choice, perhaps dedicated to the planet who rules your purpose. (You may prefer joss sticks, or vaporising oil or even scented flowers. Whichever you use you should be aware of its symbolism.) Carry the scent clockwise round the circle, asking in your own words that the Sacred Breath of Life will cleanse, bless and dedicate the circle to your purpose. Replace it at the East.

Go to the South of the altar and with a taper light the candle or lamp from the central flame, snuff out the taper, then carry the lamp clockwise round the circle, saying words to the effect of, 'May the energy of this Holy Light cleanse, bless and dedicate this circle . . .'. Put the lamp back on the Southern side of the altar.

Go to the West, pick up the dish of water and walk round the circle, sprinkling a few drops in each direction as you go, either with your fingers or a sprig of some appropriate tree or herb. Say, 'May the waters of Love cleanse, bless, and dedicate this circle . . .'.

Then finally go to the North, pick up the stone or pentacle, carry it round clockwise saying,' May the mighty power of Law cleanse, bless and dedicate this circle – now and forever more'.

Return to the East side of the altar. Take the new item you wish to bless, unwrap it from the clean cloth it should be enclosed in and carefully pass it through the incense smoke, asking that the element of air will cleanse it, breathe magical life into it and dedicate it to your purpose, that is its future occult use.

Repeat this with fire, water and the stone. You can use rock salt as a symbol of earth (not sea salt!) and sprinkle that over the item and around the circle, if you don't mind the grains on the carpet.

Every magical thing you intend to use, Tarot cards, your robe, cord and sandals, the candles for the next ritual, any dishes or bowls, the book in which you record all your workings, even, should be individually dedicated and made sacred in this way.

There are several ways of consecrating the circle at the beginning of any working. One is to start in the East with air, then South with fire, then West with water, and finally North and earth, which allows the highest and most subtle, invisible spiritual energy to descend through more and more dense elements. This method is usually followed in lodges of ritual magicians as the most senior is generally in the East, although the other three positions are often held by the individual with the most ability in dealing with the particular element. The other way, often better for a novice working alone or with other trainees, is to begin with the symbol of Earth in the North, then West, then South and finally East. In each case the symbol is picked up and carried clockwise round the altar, three-quarters of a circle, so that in the end you have completed three whole circles. At the end of any ritual the reverse circling anti-clockwise with each element will close down the energy raised and return the place to normal.

If you are not in a position to have actual cups and candles in your room then you will have to seek out something as simple as picture postcards which represent the elements. For example, a country view of trees, fields and farmland could be placed on the North wall; a picture of the sea, a lake or river or even an elaborate goblet be used for the West. Find a bonfire-night scene or fireworks for the South and a view of sunrise, mist or clouds and mountain peaks to stand for elemental Air. These need not be too obvious, if you are not in a position to share your interests with the rest of your household. However, try to be open and honest about this as the distrust, even within a family, can weaken your magic, and cause unpleasant atmospheres just when you need to feel calm and confident. If you meditate on any such problems a real and lasting solution will 'pop into your mind' in the way that all 'realisations' do, so that you have an effective way of reassuring those around you, or of coping with any practical problems. It is worth the effort of doing this at the start of your potentially life-long interest so that all difficulties are sorted out and may never bother you again.

9 · COMPANIONS ON THE PATH

Slowly, the trainee magician comes to realise that he or she is alone on the Path. No matter how many fellow pupils there may be in one's Occult School, no matter how close the bond between student and teacher, no two spiritual quests are the same. We are seeking different things . . . . or more confusingly, seeking different answers to the *same* questions. . . .

Magick and the Tarot
Tony Willis

The ideal situation in all magical training is that you get in touch with a ritual Order or a coven of witches which meets near your home and which, at precisely the moment you start looking for companions, happens also to be seeking new members. You apply and are welcomed with open arms into a group who will become closer than your own blood relations! That is the ideal – it is seldom met with in this life or on this planet.

The actual number of real magical Orders, run by people with experience, compassion and power can be counted on the fingers of one hand: Reputable covens, though a good deal more numerous are no easier to find, especially by untrained novices who have no idea of what they might be letting themselves in for. The number of 'Black Magic' groups within the framework of real magic is *NIL*. However, there are a few perverted and evil organisations which allege to be magical, but have nothing to do with genuine occult groups. For this reason, do be very careful if you are answering an advert in a paper which is not run by a reputable esoteric publisher, especially if you are under twenty-five, or female, or totally alone in your studies with no wise soul to advise you. If you have any doubts, do *not* get involved, and should you realise that a group which is trying to recruit you is using drugs, bondage, sexual practices or seeks very young people, please report this, anonymously if you prefer, to the police.

I will say this very firmly because I know it to be a fact through nearly thirty years' practical involvement with occult groups in Britain, Ireland, the USA and parts of Europe: real magicians and witches, of all paths, are highly *ethical, moral* and *responsible people*. Their work is serving the *Light of Creation*, by healing, self-awareness and rediscovery of our magical heritage of beneficial powers. They are in no way involved in harming animals or people, performing curses, initiating teenagers or younger folk, nor forcing individuals to participate in taking drugs or other unacceptable practices. Their work is to bring humanity forward through our long evolution, by raising consciousness and conforming with the highest principles and morals within individual seekers.

It is difficult to gain personal instruction, although in the last few years more and more of the teachers and writers on Western Esoteric subjects are devoting time to running day courses of instruction in many parts of Britain, Europe and the USA. The reason is that an intensive short course in the presence of an experienced ritualist, witch or magician can set in train the inner abilities of every individual student. The arts of magic are essentially simple. They mainly involve the controlled change in consciousness achieved through regular meditation, creative visualisation and inner journeying, the understanding of the power of myth and symbol and consistent effort to master self-awareness, inner confidence and personal growth. The rest is stage dressing and psychological support systems. Each of the above mental and psychic skills has to be mastered by each individual, as an individual. A group can only share some of the external work and offer companionship. They cannot learn for you, do your 'homework' for you, or bring enlightenment to you in a handy, ready-to-use package, any more than they can drink water for you, or take on the boring exercises of learning the piano or a foreign language for you. If you want magical power, *you* will have to work for it.

The most obvious source of magical instruction is books. Today there are many excellent new works being produced every year, written by experienced practical magicians, witches and occult philosophers. But it isn't just a matter of getting a new title and glancing through it, turning to the most advanced exercises at the back, trying these once or twice in a desultory or careless fashion, getting no tangible results, and either declaring 'All magic is bunk!' or telling all and sundry that you are now the Grand High Magnifico-Magus of the Whole Universe and expecting people not to laugh in your face! Magic requires work. It requires dedication. It requires consistent, regular and determined persistence, over weeks, months, years or the rest of your life. It will repay vast dividends, in spiritual and eternal currency, though on the material plane, occultists of all paths find they have sufficient rather than a fortune. Their treasure is counted in the friends they have and maintain, the respect they inspire in the people they come into contact with, both magical and mundane, the way they are able to solve life's problems in non-destructive ways. They gain love and trust and the ability to work in harmony with others, and that is a prize above gold.

The companionship you might find in any group, pagan or high magic, will have a profound effect upon you. Jung described the idea of the Collective Unconscious, wherein everyone's memories and experiences are stored, and which may be consulted by trained occultists. Any group of like-minded people who come together for a common purpose produce a similar effect, called the Group Mind, which influences those who come under its aegis. This may be true within a school, or a football club, but it happens to a far greater effect in any esoteric gathering. Those who are fully established create a kind of inner pattern and those who are introduced to the group through initiation will find that they are changed by the experience. Part of the many-faceted changes that any true initiation brings is the combined effect of the Group Mind of the existing membership and their inner plane teachers or 'contacts'. Not everyone enjoys this experience, for it can be very unsettling.

One of the most common side-effects of any kind of magical work is an increased awareness, particularly on the emotional level. Your feelings and your sensitivity to those around you is suddenly, and often unpleasantly, delicate. Whereas before, as an 'ordinary' person, you might have felt a little sympathy for others, outwardly shared their grief or joy perhaps, suddenly you find that you are profoundly affected by harsh words, or the reaction of other people. If you express your interest or practical involvement in magic you may get laughed at, and it hurts. Your new pagan religious ideals may be mocked, and

117

PRACTICAL TECHNIQUES OF MODERN MAGIC

those close to you look at you in a different and unsettling way. It is all part of the process of evolution.

As you grow into your new enlarged magical self you will have to split the skin of your previous mundane self, and this can be very tough armour, acquired during a long life of defensive thinking. Sharply this protection for the soft underbelly of your feelings is ripped away, like a dressing from a sore wound, and your nerve endings are exposed. You will find strong attractions to other members of the group you are joining, perhaps, or a feeling of almost hero-worshipping your teacher. You might find that the scoffing of your spouse or family at your new-found interest is uncomfortable, but you are not in any position to discuss your feelings about your new status as a 'witch' or initiate with non-members. You will certainly gain support from other members of the group who have been through similar traumas, but even they cannot ease your pain or prevent you sensing powerful feelings. It is part of your growth towards your perfected self, and growing pains do wear off!

Another facet of magical work is the strange and closely formed relationships between members of the group. It is not plain friendship, it goes beyond that, nor is it necessarily a sexual relationship. There is a strong and binding kinship among magical groups of all kinds which is beyond explanation until you have had personal experience of it. If you allow it, it can become obsessive, and wise teachers will watch out for unhealthy associations forming, but it will also affect relationships outside the magical group. These fall under the spotlight of your newly awoken senses and may not seem as ideal as they did before. You have to learn to live with that too. You cannot expect your partner to change to suit you, give up the comfiest chair in the warmest space so that you can hog it for your daily meditations. Nor can you opt out of family chores because you need to study or perform solo rites. Your responsibility to your existing situation is a vital part of your life, and cannot just be dropped because you have taken up a new 'hobby'. Commitments are not like old suits of clothes, to be discarded when some interesting new fashion comes your way. That too is a lesson of magic; paying the debts of your earlier life, sorting out the relationships and responsibilities, even if they are illuminated brightly by your recently discovered inner sight and all the more startling for that.

Magic is a long-term and serious commitment, not a fad to be played with for a few weeks until a more exciting interest comes along. It is for this reason that most of the best magical schools have basic training courses, often run by postal tuition, lasting from one to four years! During that time you will master the basic individual arts, read much of the chosen mythology, understand the structure, patterns and symbols of your tradition, and be really ready for admission to a working group.

At every stage of your training you must assess your own progress, and heartfelt honesty is vital here. You alone will be judging how clear your meditation realisations become, and how frequent (this is the occult equivalent of an orgasm!) and how you can make these happen when you need them! It is no good boasting to others about your revelations; those inner messages are for you alone, to train and extend your skills. You need to develop a good memory, patience, fortitude when things seem to go wrong, and the controlled sensitivity which allows you to be aware of the pain caused to and by other people, but which helps you cope also. There really are no short cuts, no matter what some manual advertised in the press might suggest. You wouldn't expect to be able to play the cello like a maestro in one lesson, would you, or speak Portuguese like a native without months of practice? Magic is the same and takes the same kind of perseverance and dedication, but then, with magic, the sky is the limit!

You will also need to develop particular skills of creativity and handicrafts, so that you can write meaningful prayers and invocations, sew comfortable robes, embroider altar cloths, or paint wall hangings. You might take up pottery to make your cup and platter, or wood carving or metal work at evening classes. You might choose to study ancient history, mythology or languages, or travel to visit sacred sites both far and near, steeping yourself in their essence and recreating it within your inner journeys. You may become a poet, or a priest or a ruler of those inner realms, if you are so inspired.

You might like to work with the masks and head-dresses of ancient Egypt and her many powerful animal-headed Gods and Goddesses. You might learn to drum or chant for shamanic rites, or sing new songs in the oldest way, taught directly by the inspiration of the wind in the trees or the water falling in Nature's own garden. You may, with your own hands, build a real temple, with its starry floor cloth or piebald tiles, its double cube altar, its lofty pillars, black and silver, crowned with light and elegant tracery. You may set out thrones for the officers, carved with mystic symbols, or have Quarter banners, each displaying its strange device. You might create statues of your deities, or make for them a scented garden, a wild woodland glade, a sacred enclosure, on this plane or any other.

119

There are many gifts of the Unseen Ones, of inspiration, exhilaration and joy, of intuition and certainty, of poetry and words of comfort, of acceptance and divination or healing skill. Within you is all potential. You alone are in the position of being able to set it free, guided by your inner resources, through traditional ritual, new magic and ancient arts.

CLOSING AND BENEDICTION

Blessed are they who set out upon an Endless Quest,
Blessed are they who walk in Darkness, seeking Light,
Blessed are they who, abandoning all worldly things, seek out the Gates
of Paradise
That they may lead all beings to their rightful home.

Grail Catechism
The Grail Seeker's Companion
John Matthews & Marian Green

Magic is concerned with change, recognising it, willing it into being
and controlling it. At one level, all aspects of change are within
the magician and his ritual is the vehicle of initiating the change
and holding it in his will. Whatever the purpose of any ritual, at
least part of its effects will be upon the magician, causing him to
change, to grow and to see the world through new eyes. One false
or unwise move can set in train a sequence of events which can
have serious and far-reaching consequences, and the ritualist, no
matter how green or inexperienced, will ultimately be responsible
for those future events. Before any act of ritual magic, it is therefore
wise to reflect long and hard on the possible outcomes; not only the
desired result, but any imbalances which might be set toppling, like
dominoes, in an unstoppable tumble.

Before you seek initiation or make rash promises of eternal dedication to the Path, be wary. Magic is a hard master, its arts are endless and the work lifelong. Though you may feel you have a vocation for the sacred and arcane studies you also have a position in the world, a home to keep, a family perhaps, and a job. Magic will not solve any of your problems, it will simply magnify your sensitivity so that what seems insoluble now will pale into insignificance when you perceive the burden of the Earth's problems which, through your shared kinship with all sentient life, becomes your burden too. Magic is not a short cut, a cop-out from the responsibilities of the world. The ritual temple is not a cosy retreat from the passions and confusions of the round of everyday life. It is a forge and a furnace wherein you will be battered and remoulded, dissolved and re-formed through the painful processes of personal evolution and spiritual growth.

The magical arts of ritual are eternal and its working is beyond time. Those who do dedicate themselves to these ancient skills of mind and soul and body may be taking up an old wisdom whose seeds were sown in them many lives ago, completing the unfinished work, the unfulfilled commitments, the broken promises, to bring to conclusion those tasks that even the centuries have not eaten away.

By opening the doors to the inner mind through the gentle arts of meditation, contemplation and creative visualisation, and sharing the companionship of others within the lodge or coven or grove, great steps forward in humanity's shared heritage may be made, even now at the technological end of the twentieth century. The arts we recall now, the skills and abilities which we may each reclaim, will lay down a firm and magical foundation for the era that is dawning. As we who are students now become the teachers in the next turn of the cosmic spiral, we will ensure that the highest aspiration of the human soul will be tended, and those inner longings will be satisfied, for our experiences will be their nourishment, protection and blessing in the age to come.

There is a blessing on all who serve . . .

Marian Green
Bristol, March 1989

· BIBLIOGRAPHY

There are literally hundreds of new and reissued books of practical magic and ritual. Most of the authors listed below have written several other titles, and all the publishers will be pleased to send up-to-date lists of their books, if you write and ask. Public libraries keep complete lists of all books in print under various headings, and from that data you should be able to get your local bookshop to order your chosen titles.

Dolores Ashcroft-Nowicki, *Highways of the Mind*, Aquarian Press, 1987 *First Steps in Ritual*, Aquarian Press, 1982

J.H. Brennan, *Experimental Magic*, Aquarian Press, 1984

W.E. Butler, *Apprenticed to Magic*, Crucible 1979, *Magic: Its Ritual, Power & Purpose*, Aquarian Press, 1952

A. Crowley, *Magick in Theory and Practice*, Dover, USA, 1986

J. & S. Farrar, *The Witches' Way*, Robert Hale, 1984

Dion Fortune, *Esoteric Orders and Their Work*, Aquarian Press, 1987 *Applied Magic*, Aquarian Press, 1987

W.G. Gray, *Magical Ritual Methods*, Aquarian Press, 1980

Marian Green, *Magic for the Aquarian Age*, Aquarian Press, 1983 *Experiments in Aquarian Magic*, Aquarian Press, 1985 *The Gentle Arts of Aquarian Magic*, Aquarian Press, 1987

(with John Matthews), *The Grail Seeker's Companion*, Aquarian Press, 1986 *The Path through the Labyrinth*, Element Books, 1988 *The Elements of Natural Magic*, Element Books, 1989

Helene Hess, *The Zodiac Explorer's Guide*, Aquarian Press, 1986

Murry Hope, *Practical Techniques of Psychic Self Defence*, Aquarian Press, 1983 *Practical Egyptian Magic*, Aquarian Press, 1985 *The Psychology of*

Ritual, Element Books, 1988 *Practical Greek Magic*, Aquarian Press, 1985
Naomi Humphrey, *Meditation: The Inner Way*, Aquarian Press, 1987
Caitlin Matthews, *The Elements of the Celtic Tradition*, Element Books, 1989
John & Caitlin Matthews, *The Western Way* (2 vols.), Arkana (RKP), 1984
Will Parfitt, *The Living Qabalah*, Element Books, 1988
R.J.Stewart, *Advanced Magical Arts*, Element Books, 1988
Doreen Valiente, *Witchcraft for Tomorrow*, Robert Hale, 1978
Tony Willis, *The Runic Workbook*, Aquarian Press, 1986 *Magick and the Tarot*,
    Aquarian Press, 1988

· NOTE

Marian also runs correspondence courses and gives talks and practical training to small groups throughout Britain, Europe, and Canada. She has also issued a number of instructional and path-working cassette tapes.

If you are interested in contacting the author about the talks and correspondence courses she runs, please write to her care of the publishers;

Thoth Publications
98 Ashby Road
Loughborough
Leicestershire LE11 3AF

(please include a stamped addressed envelope)

INDEX